Maci's Place

The Loss of a Child through a Father's Eyes

By
Michael S. Miller

E-BookTime, LLC
Montgomery, Alabama

Maci's Place
The Loss of a Child through a Father's Eyes

ISBN: 978-1-60862-683-0

Second Edition
Published March 2017
E-BookTime, LLC
6598 Pumpkin Road
Montgomery, AL 36108
www.e-booktime.com

For Lisa,
my loving wife, who never stopped
supporting me
and believing in me.

"The Nameless Few"

When your husband dies, you become a widow.
When your wife dies, a widower. Children who
lose their parents are called orphans. But we have
no name for the parent who loses a child.

In loving memory of my little angel
Maci Danielle Miller
February 5, 1994 – May 12, 2001

Contents

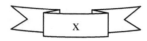

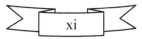

Contents

Preface

For many years, it has been my New Year's Resolution to write a book on how men – specifically Dad's – deal with the loss of a child.

As I began writing this book, I began experiencing and reliving the emotions I felt the day I received that dreadful call. For every chapter and each line of this book, I have strived to focus my attention towards ways that I could make a positive difference in someone's life.

I am not a doctor, nurse, psychiatrist, psychologist, grief counselor, or even have a medical degree for that matter. I do not claim to be a subject matter expert in matters of grief. What I am is a dad who lost his daughter far before her time, and has had to deal with the everyday blows that life tends to offer.

As I struggled through the first few years of my loss, I felt as if I were grasping for straws. I went to professionals like doctors and counselors, but I just did not get the answers I was looking for. Obviously, there are questions we will never have the answers to, but my initial questions seemed so obvious at the time.

I recall going to visit a Psychiatrist. The first question that came out of his mouth was, "What would you like to get

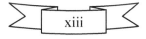

from our visits?" I was floored to say the least. I was hoping he could tell me how to make it through this time of grief.

How do I find the energy to get up every morning?

How do I stop seeing the pictures of my daughter on her deathbed?

How can I possibly go to sleep at night?

When I did sleep, how do I cease having the disturbing dreams? I had so many questions, yet no one to answer.

There are some great books that have been published about losing a child, but none specific for us dads. Therefore, that is the reason I have begun this quest.

I was asked not too long ago how long it had been since I lost my daughter. At that time, it had been a little over six years. However, there are days when it seems like it happened yesterday. It is in those days that I have to reach deep inside and go to the place that helped me the first few years.

For everyone, that place will be different. It may be your child's bedroom. It may be a special place you visited together. It may be a church. It might be a visit through the countless memorabilia we have collected and saved through the years.

For me, it is the reminder of the ritual my daughter and I shared after every phone call. Before hanging up or passing the phone to her brother, we would always say, "Hugs and Kisses" and make the sound you would get if being given a bear hug followed by a "smooch."

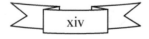

It is those very special moments that I have tucked away in my heart for the "rainy days" I still experience. I call it Maci's Place.

Introduction

Grief offers no explanations. No one seems to understand how you feel, let alone those that try and provide some comfort. While it is incredibly painful to relive memories and to ask the dreaded question of why, this book has been designed to offer inspiration and to let you know that you are far from alone in your quest for answers.

This book offers hope and provides information. Hopefully it will open a door in your heart that will allow pain to be melted away by the true love you feel for your child. Here, I outline the true story of one man's loss in the hope that it provides comfort and understanding to you. In addition, it outlines the psychology behind the way you feel day in and day out. By journeying through this firsthand experience, you will also maneuver your way through the process and understand why things are happening the way that they are.

This book will help others to heal, not just by the science included, but also by the fact of knowing that you are not alone in your journey.

This book is intended for men, suffering from the loss of their child, in any number of situations. Yet, if you are a loved one trying to understand what is happening to the man in your life, it can provide guidance as well. Through the detailed explanations here, I hope that those that want to understand the way a man truly feels with such great loss will understand just how incredibly painful it can be.

There is no way to wipe clean the slate and take back these days to the day when your child was still alive, running into your arms. There is no way to stop missing and to stop hurting. Yet, you can move from today until tomorrow and slowly begin to structure your life in the way that your child wanted you to.

You will never replace them in your heart, and you don't want to. But, you can learn to remember them with love rather than pain.

A Letter to My Angel

Hello my little angel
I'm just writing to see how you've been.
It's hard to believe it's been four months
Since I last held your little hand.

I guess you wonder if you ever cross my mind
Well, at least a million times a day.
It seems like everything I touch and see
Reminds me of you in every way.

It might just be a toy on the shelf
Or the passing of a ladybug.
Oh, if I could just have one more moment with you
Just to give you one last hug.

I am sure you are a beautiful angel
And in the choir you get to sing.
I bet you have the biggest halo,
I'd give anything to see your wings.

I know you are in a better place
Heaven has streets of gold and crystal water.
But my heaven on earth was taken from me
When you were taken, my precious daughter.

So, if it's not too much to ask
And if you really wouldn't mind
Could you take a little trip to earth
To check on your daddy from time to time?

Well, I guess I should be going now
Pardon the tears that stain this note.
I hope you can feel my love for you
In every letter of every word I wrote.

I love you and miss you baby!
"Kisses and Hugs"
Daddy
September 29, 2001

xx

Chapter 1

The Call

It was a little after 7 PM May 11, 2001.

I was at a rehearsal dinner having a great time and celebrating a time of happiness with some friends when my cell phone rang. I was living in Virginia at the time, and the call was originating from Indiana. Although I have family in Indiana, we did not speak much by phone. When I answered the phone, I was surprised to hear my ex mother-in-laws voice.

She informed me that my son and daughter and their mother had been involved in a car accident. She did not have any details, but she provided me the name and number of the attending physician. As she was telling me the news, I was scrambling for a pen to take the number. Finally, the server handed me a marker in which I was able to take down the number. As quickly as possible, I went outside to make the call to the physician.

It seemed like I was on hold for hours, although it was only a couple of minutes. I was not prepared for what I was about to hear.

Although it is still kind of a blur, these are the words I remember the doctor saying to me: "Your son and daughter have been involved in a serious head on collision. Your daughter has internal bleeding. I tried to operate, but the bleeding is too severe. We need her blood pressure to drop so I can go back in. She went into cardiac arrest in the ambulance and once while she was in surgery."

This is when I fell to the ground and began sobbing. The doctor continued. "We are doing all we can for your daughter. However, she only has about 20% chance of surviving."

At this point, I thought I was going to be sick. I became nauseated and light headed. She continued. "I had to perform emergency surgery on your son. I took out about three inches of damaged intestines. He had a compound fracture of his wrist, and we have….." Then it just seemed that I was catching bits and pieces at this time. The last I remember her saying was that Michael's chances of surviving were much better.

The only thing I can recall saying is, "I am getting on a plane and will be there tonight." Somewhere in that conversation, I asked about their mother, but she had been taken to another hospital and the doctor did not have a status.

People who have gone through a loss of a child say that particular point in time is a pivotal point in our lives. Everything we do for the rest of our lives revolve around the date before and after we lost our child.

As I dropped to the ground and began to sob uncontrollably, I thought that I was going to die. I had never felt the excruciating pain I was experiencing.

God truly does work in mysterious ways, and he says he will never give us more than we can bear. However, at that moment in time, had I known the level of pain and hurt I was to experience in the days ahead, I am not sure if my heart, body, mind and soul would have been able to withstand it.

Chapter 2

Men and Fear

Sometime during the course of their upbringing men, become conditioned to believe that they should never show that they are afraid of anything. In fact, they could be trembling with fear, but it must never show on the outside.

It does not matter if the topic is facing uncertainty or facing your first date; men are told, encouraged and even ridiculed if they show that they are afraid. For some men, the need to hide such feelings is even put on themselves.

Society may not encourage men to be afraid, and whether or not you believe they should or not, the fact is that fear is a rational, human instinct. It helps us to realize that the situation is dangerous, in some form. It helps us to take care of what we do next to protect us, emotionally, mentally and physically.

The science behind this is simple. During high anxiety times, including times when fear comes rushing in, the individual's body must do all it can to be ready for the instant when all attention must be on the problem. Our hearts begin to beat faster and heavier, forcing more oxygen to the brain and to each of your limbs. You can move faster, react faster and you can respond to the situation in the best way possible.

Fear also has an emotional stronghold on your situation. When fear begins to take charge, the mind is also racing. As that oxygen flows to your brain, the questions develop in an effort to plan for the worst.

What if I don't make the right decision?

What will happen to me if something happens to my daughter?

What if the worst possible thing happens and I can't make it stop?

Fear, anxiety and even stress add to the physical toll of any situation. In many cases, such as these extreme situations when your mind and body are racing, your body is simply preparing yourself for the worst situation so that when it hits, it does not hurt as much. Of course, this is not always a possible outcome.

Society's Role in Men's Fears

Society often looks down on men that actually show emotion, let alone fear. This very real, very human emotion is one that every person in the world feels, from time to time and there is no hiding it.

Yet, if you were to walk through an area mall and you saw a man sitting on a bench crying, weeping...you would likely be in awe. Tears rolling down your father's eyes mean that something is very wrong as "men just don't cry."

Fear is the same way. Men supposedly should not show this emotion because it shows weakness. Although fear is anything but weakness, people often do not realize just how powerful of an emotion it is. If you did not care about the situation, you would likely not be afraid. If you did not care about the outcome, you wouldn't have sweaty palms and a racing mind.

Men Are Problem Solvers

Part of the problem that society has when it comes to men expressing feelings is the very real fact that men are supposed to be the problem solvers in our world. Men start wars, but men finish them. Men created the Constitution and men signed it. Men save women from burning buildings. Men are heroes. Men are the problem solver.

In other words, a man cannot solve problems if he is afraid and therefore, he should never show such weakness.

That statement may be the way society treats men and what it expects from a man, yet it is anything from the truth. There is science to back it up, even.

The fact is that fear is a very powerful emotion that drives us to do more and to be more. Your body is giving all it has to provide your mind and your physical body with all of the necessary resources to battle the situation at hand. Like going into war, it is putting on its armor and preparing for the fight.

Likewise, your emotions are doing the same thing. In fear, men can experience the true situation clearer and although

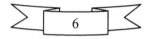

tears may be in their eyes, their hearts are encouraging their heads to find a solution.

In situations like such devastating grief, it becomes very important for the man to tuck away his emotions and to develop themselves into a warrior, ready to find the problem and solve it. Yet, in grief, there is no simple solution, nor a complex one.

Your Forbidden Grief

When your child is no longer there to hold out their hand for you to hold or for you to scold for saying the wrong thing at the wrong time, grief becomes a part of you. As a man, you may feel that you are unable to grieve, but it is completely natural for you to do so.

All men will grieve in their unique way; some will grieve openly allowing the world to console them. Others will avoid anything to do with that grief, pushing it aside.

Fear and grief are elements you may not want to deal with on a regular basis but the fact is you will deal with it. You may lose your temper for no reason. You may find yourself lost in thought when you see a small girl riding her bike down the street. You may just find yourself not looking forward to doing things with your family and friends. Or, the things you used to enjoy may no longer matter to you.

Fear of the unknown whether it be how you will make it to the next day or how you will confront what the doctor has to say, will be a part of your everyday life. Every person will deal with their grief in their own way. You'll see fear and grief jump into your life, but it may become less often as time moves on.

What Really Is Okay?

As a man, it is difficult to believe it, but being afraid is something that is acceptable. It does not matter what the world around you sees in you or believes about you. In fact, a man is only as strong as he allows himself to become, and being afraid is a way of defining yourself.

Cry when you need to cry. If you can't do so in public or with family, lock the door to the bathroom and cry. Let the tears run down your face under the hot shower where no one sees it. Scream to your heart's content in exasperation when you are terrified of what tomorrow holds. Go to the gym, grab some boxing gloves and pound that bag imagining it to be all the frustration, fear and grief within.

There are benefits to letting all out, so to speak. When you are afraid of what tomorrow holds, express that form of grief. When you do, you open the door and let it out, letting it escape your mind and your body. Finding a way to release yourself will allow you to push it aside, even just for a short time, so that you can get on with the day.

The only thing to avoid is destructive behavior that will hurt yourself or others. Expressing your fears in other ways is by far acceptable and necessary.

Chapter 3

The Airport

Time stands still so much so that time becomes the enemy…

Within five minutes of the call, I was in the car and heading home to pack. I am not sure how I even made travel arrangements, but I believe I called my parents who acted on my behalf. I do not remember that 30 minute ride home. I do not remember even packing. It was not until I arrived in Louisville, Kentucky that I realized I packed the bare minimum which did not include a suit. After all, what would I need a suit for?

It could not have taken more than 10 minutes to pack. I was back in the car and heading to Dulles Airport to catch a late flight to Louisville. I believe it was at that time that my dad called me and gave me the times of my flight. I remember looking at my watch and thinking I would never make it.

I kept looking at my watch. I kept thinking, "My God, I am never going to make it. It is the last flight of the night. My kids need me." I then began to say a small prayer. "Please God, let me catch this flight."

I arrived at the airport and did not even take time to park in long-term parking. I rushed through the doors to find all of the ticket counters closed. I finally found someone who worked for the airline I was flying on, and they said I would have to purchase the tickets at the gate.

My heart was sinking with each and every passing second. I remember telling her it was an emergency and to see if she could make sure the plane did not leave. Not only did she say she could not do anything about it, but the suitcase I was carrying might not be small enough to get through security. Once again, I felt the nausea and light headed feelings. I began to run for the gates.

Luckily, this was about four months prior to the 9/11 event, so security was not as tight as it is today. There was no one else in line. I have never seen an airport look so empty and desolate. I breezed through security and continued to run for the gates. The entire time I was just praying that I would make it before it pulled away.

When I arrived at the gate, there were many people sitting around which made me believe they were either on the same flight as me, or waiting for another flight. I ran to the ticket counter and informed the attendant that I had a family emergency and needed to buy a ticket for the Louisville flight. I remember begging her to please make sure I got on that flight.

It was a sense of relief when she said there were plenty of seats and gave me my boarding pass.

For the first time since the call, I sat down and wiped away the combination of sweat and tears that had been flowing down my face continuously for the past couple of hours.

I began to replay the phone conversation in my head. I placed my head in my hands and began to weep ever so quietly.

After all, I was a man and I was supposed to be strong. I had served almost 12 years in the army and was a combat veteran. I was not supposed to show any signs of weakness.

"Be a man, Mike. Get a hold of yourself."

Chapter 4

When You Can't Be Strong

Strength is a term many men hold on a pedestal. The stronger you are, the less likely you are to be defeated, broken or otherwise harmed. Strength wins wars and wins battles with any demon. For that reason, men don't cry.

When a male cries, he is looked down upon as if it is a sign of weakness. The culture around you makes this happen, time and time again. In many cultures, including European cultures, Australian cultures, Asian cultures and especially American cultures, men are taught from a young age that they are not to cry. "Boys don't cry." "Real men never cry."

If you cry, you lose face. In some cultures, men are taught that crying is shameful. It is that way in the German culture and in the Norwegian culture. If you cry, people will feel contempt for you.

Men still feel the emotions that crying brings out. The fear, anxiety and of course the sadness still must come out in some form. People express themselves like this. Yet, many men work very hard at suppressing their emotions.

If a man does cry, he may even feel the need to apologize for it. "I'm sorry, I was weak." Or, "I'm sorry for breaking down." Some feel disgraced by the entire situation, and in some situations, a family may even encourage a young male to apologize or to feel like this.

In other cultures, for example in South Africa, and in some situations with Mexican and Latin American cultures, men do cry. In fact, men cry openly in many situations. They do not hold back, nor do they feel any remorse for doing so. They are not looked down upon, nor are they belittled for doing so.

It is in these cultures that you are able to see, clearly, that crying is a part of the normal emotional scheme and is expected behavior.

In some societies, people are studying the effects of not expressing emotion, which is what you would be doing if you do not allow yourself to try. Suppressed emotions, such as crying, force negative energy into your body. In some cases, it has been seen that the more suppressed an individual is, the more likely he is to face larger illnesses in life.

The author of one book, entitled, *Why We Get Sick And How We Get Well*, named Janov, is a believer in such situations.

Another book to consider is *The Journey: A Practical Guide To Healing Your Life And Setting Yourself Free*, by Brandon Bays. In fact, in this book the author relates her story on how she was able to cure herself of a large tumor after examining the real problem behind the tumor, which she determined was suppressed anger.

Whether you believe in such things or not is not what is important, though. What is, is fully understanding where you are today in terms of crying. Crying will allow the healing process to begin. Cry, in a bathroom stall or in the car on the way home. Cry where you feel you can. Just do not suppress it.

How Men Face Helplessness

There will be many times within your life that you feel helpless. What can you do? Why can't you do anything? The loss of a child is one such situation. Being helpless is something most men cannot tolerate, though.

For example, you are unable to help your very ill child. You stand there, look at them and feel the need to do something. Why can't you do something?

In some situations, men will begin to look for other ways to use themselves in the hopes of being helpful. For example, you may find it necessary to take care of the bills, take care of your family or even get back to work so that your career does not falter. You are taking care of something even if you feel helpless. Many men use this coping mechanism.

As you sit there, waiting for time to move so that you get to your child, you make plans about what you will do to fix the situation. Men cannot just remain helpless; they have to find a way to fix the problem. And, when you cannot fix the situation, men can easily spiral out of control.

In comparison, when a woman breaks down and cries, she may be more readily able to and willing to rely on someone to help her through the process. While she feels helpless, she is able to be okay with that long enough for the healing process to begin. With a man, there is no acknowledgement of such feelings, which will push them further into the depths of despair.

All of these reactions are very normal and really are to be expected by a man that is faced with such tragic and horrific situations such as losing your child. Helplessness is something most men cannot comprehend or communicate. Understanding that it is a normal human emotion brought on by tragic situations allows you to feel okay about feeling this way, even if you do not express those feelings otherwise.

Dealing with Emotions You Don't Know How to Handle

How do people go through life with the weight of their child's death on their shoulders? As you look around a public location, you may find yourself asking, "How can they be so happy?" "What gives them the right to live a happy life?"

You may find all types of emotions spitting up from deep within. Sadness, helplessness, anxiety, terror, and anger are just a handful of these. Since many men feel that they can't express these emotions, they will suppress them, deeply in some situations.

When suppression of emotions happens, those emotions can take on other forms. For example, not giving in to feeling helpless and devastated may drive a man to work more because he feels that this is something he can control and do well at. That may sound good until his marriage falls apart because he cannot remember the last time he saw his wife.

In other situations, suppression of emotions can lead to physical and mental difficulties and illnesses. Anxiety and stress weighs heavily on the body, causing all types of illnesses including heart disease. On the flip side, emotional trauma that goes without being dealt with can result in additional problems including depression which is a life threatening condition.

So, how can you deal with these emotions if you are not willing to lose face and cry? How can you get past the troubled images and thoughts you have without showing these raw images to the public?

There are many ways to do so, and you will need to find an outlet to help you to do so. Later in this book, we will outline some of the best methods for dealing with pent up emotions including anger, frustration, helplessness and profound sadness.

A few ideas until then include those that we've mentioned such as:

- Let out your tears in private. A good cry can help you to gain clarity and preserve your mind set.

- Head to the gym and work out the tension and anger you feel by directing it at a punching bag.

- If you find yourself depressed or unable to cope with day to day life, seek out the help of a professional. Many men do this without anyone knowing they are and reap the rewards without dealing with any consequences.

Of course, it is important to point out that there is nothing wrong with expressing your emotions outright. You do not have to hide from people to express them. Most importantly, you can allow yourself to cry and not feel ashamed for doing so. If you cannot bring yourself to do that, though, these other methods offer some relief.

Mustering Strength for Everyone Else

One common way for men to deal with emotions is to just suppress them, put them aside or forget about them so that they can have enough strength for everyone else. This is likely to be one of the most common situations a man can be put in when it comes to dealing with the death of your child.

As a man, you may feel the need to have the strength needed to support your family and friends. You have to be there for your child's mother who is in unimaginable pain and is inconsolable. You have to be there for your child's siblings who do not understand what is happening and are also dealing with grief in the worst form. You have to be there for your own parents, who are too old and fragile to deal with such tragedy. You have to be there for....

The list can go on and on, and it is easy to see why this may be one of the best ways for a man to deal with the loss of his child. After all, when you are there for someone else, you do not have to deal with your own emotions. You can tuck them away and put the spotlight on what you feel is more important: other people.

While this may be a common way for men to handle grief and sadness, it may not be healthy. The bottom line is simple. You have lost something dear to you, too. You are the one that should have people consoling you. Most importantly, you do deserve to have someone hold you up so that you can weep in pain. These are allowable feelings even if you do not believe that they are.

For many men, this will not happen. Instead, they will push aside their feelings. If you do this, remember that you still need an outlet for those feelings so that they do not become suppressed.

Chapter 5

The Plane Ride

This was another time when I look back and details just seem to be fuzzy.

I do recall the plane not being too full, so I got my pick of seats. I remember picking a seat up front so I could be the first one off the plane. I sat down by the window, buckled up, and gazed out the window.

I don't recall my gaze ever leaving the window until we landed in Louisville.

I do remember some of the thoughts that were going through my head. I am sure for those of you who have been in similar circumstances after hearing this kind of news; you were thinking the same thoughts.

As the tears slowly streamed from my eyes, I began trying to condition myself for what I would be seeing in a few hours. I knew my son and daughter were in an Intensive Care Unit (ICU), and I was trying to picture them connected to the machines.

I was trying to create the beeping sound of the monitors.

I imagined them with breathing tubes in their noses and mouths.

I kept thinking that if I can prepare myself mentally, then I will be much stronger when I arrive. Little did I know that nothing can prepare you during that time when you see your child or children on their deathbeds.

I do recall the taxi driver not speaking very good English, and I was getting very frustrated with trying to tell him where I needed to go. I am sure he did not get too many requests to go from the airport to the Louisville Children's hospital – especially around midnight.

However, after what seemed to take longer than the plane ride, he pulled into the emergency room parking lot. He gave me my suitcase, I paid him and I ran through the emergency room (ER) doors.

When I told the ER nurse who I was and why I was there, a very nice couple walked up to me. I do not remember their names, but I do remember them telling me they were the pastor from a local church and would take me to the chaplain. I later remember thinking how wonderful it was for two complete strangers to be there to help me.

Little did I know at the time the events that had unfolded that evening and those to come, and how they were orchestrated by complete strangers. As I look back now, I see them like angels.

The pastoral couple took me to the chaplain, gave me their number, and said if there was anything I needed, to just call.

I remember dropping off the suitcase and plugging in my cell phone.

Then the chaplain said, "If you will follow me, I will take you to your kids."

Chapter 6

Conditioning for the Blow

Conditioning for the worst is one of the body's survival mechanisms. If you can imagine the worst case scenario, you can plan how to handle the situation as soon as it hits.

For example, planning to see your child with cords attached to them and hovering nurses may help you to take care of the situation and perhaps allow you to not be shocked, overwhelmed or even to "lose it."

It is a very normal reaction to try and condition yourself for what is coming. For many people, the action is something they do on a regular basis. You may prepare yourself for your upset boss or you may prepare yourself for telling your wife that you can't take that trip you've been planning.

Each of these things is a method of coping. When you hear bad news as sudden and drastic of your child's situation, you may react through this method of coping. Preparing yourself to hear the worst and to see the worst may be a normal reaction, but it is never quite capable of hitting the mark and offering any real comfort to you.

When you walk into a room and see your child fighting a battle that they never should have been fighting, that you never imagined that they would fight, there is no amount of preparation that can make that image more capable of being dealt with.

This often leaves people broken, terrified and feeling helpless. This is very difficult for any man, especially when they are used to taking care of all situations and making sure that nothing does go wrong.

How Do You Deal with Bad News?

The way that you deal with bad news says a lot about you. Do you dive into the problem and try to fix it? Or, do you step back, afraid that you may make it worse? Dealing with negative situations like this is difficult for anyone, but the way that you handle the situation is likely to say a lot about you.

For some, hearing something bad means an instant reaction of terror. Others go into denial. For example, in one situation, a man learned that his older son had become ill and that he was taken to the hospital. His wife, who had called to tell him to come, had not said what the condition was only that it was very urgent. As he hung up the phone, he became very nervous and almost scared to leave his job to go to the hospital. He would have had no problem rushing out the door but instead he took his time, terrified over what he could see and what could be wrong when he got there.

Delaying the inevitable is a common feeling when you are faced with a tragic reaction to your situation. When it is your child, lying helpless in a bed, and you know that you may never hear them laugh again, your head spins to find any way possible to fix the situation. Unfortunately, it is never that easy.

In many ways, the sight of seeing your child like this will unnerve you to the core. Even if you are a man that does not show emotion, something deep within you will pull at your heart strings to the point of breaking. Even still, you are likely to try and make it better because that is all you know how to do.

Examine the way that you handle bad news. Do you rush in and want to gather all information possible? Do you hold back some really afraid of what lies behind closed doors? You may be someone that needs help accepting that something has gone wrong. Or, you may be the silent hero that does what you need to do and tries his best to hide the real emotion playing in his heart and mind.

Preparing for the Worst

It is very common for a man to try and prepare themselves for the worst case scenario, and there are many ways to do this. You may find yourself trying to piece together a "what if this happens" scenario so that you can deal with it when it happens.

You imagine the wires tying your child down. You imagine bruises, perhaps a tube in their nose. You try and imagine the room, filled with machines that make noises and seem to be so important. You imagine the color of the walls, the way the bed looks and even imagine the doctors and nurses without a face that are standing there, watching your baby lie in that bed. You imagine it all.

Every person will do this differently, but the goal here is the same. By imagining the very worst situation, you can go through the problem here and now, when you are safe within your home, away from all of the prying eyes of those around you. You can experience the pain and worry here, where no one needs to see you go through it.

Mentally preparing yourself for the worst is a common coping mechanism. Although most people do not think about making this happen as a rational decision, other people do. Still, the goal is the same. Prepare your mind for what you will have to go through.

In most situations, you are praying with every fiber of your body that the worst case scenario will not happen. You know what it could be, and may not even dare think of that, but you hope that if you imagine the worst that the situation will be better than that.

Tucking It in to Save Face

Even though many men will go through this type of fear and frustration, they may not be willing to show these emotions on their faces. For example, the man I mentioned that was terrified of going to the hospital to find out what was wrong, busied himself in his office as long as he could, away from the prying eyes of those around him. Although he could not imagine having to actually deal with his child's situation, it would be even worse if someone were to see him in such a condition.

As a man, you feel that you cannot show your emotions, especially in a time of stress. Even though you may be terrified of what is to come, you may be unwilling or unable even to show these emotions. As mentioned before, this is a common situation for many men from Western countries where they simply are taught not to show these signs of emotion. While it may be necessary to consider this as a normal thing, it really does not have to be like this.

Going against society is just fine and it is going to help you to prepare yourself for a better outcome. Perhaps the most important word for this section is the word, "Fear" and all that it stands for. A man feels he cannot express fear and though that may be the case, it is going to hold back your feelings and therefore cause you incredible harm in the process.

Imagine for a moment that you were to show that you were afraid of what lied behind that closed door. As a method of preparing yourself, your heart begins to ache and you do cry. You cry because you are worried, afraid and even terrified that you cannot fix the problem that your child may be injured or hurt beyond your control. If you let these emotions out now, you may be able to deal with them better.

Instead of pushing them back out of the way, as many men are likely to do, allow them to come out. You will feel as if a weight has been lifted off your shoulders if you simply talk to those that are able to help you and to share your thoughts and concerns with them. Most importantly, your mind is able to go through the situations easier, planning better for what is to come.

Although you may not do so, grabbing a loved one and crying will help you to handle the situation better simply because the emotion is out of your body. Allowing your body to handle this now will make the process better later.

Nevertheless, realize that it is very common for men to hide these fears and to never show any sign of emotion as they move to see their child or to deal with the situation at hand. There are many, many times when you will want to run and hide, and you should do so, so that you can deal with your emotions the best way you know how.

Coping with It All

As you prepare yourself for what is to come, you are likely to deal with a wide range of emotions. You will deal with frustration that you cannot be at the location where the incident is happening fast enough. You will deal with anxiety and not being able to know the outcome. Having to wait for someone else to tell you what is happening is unnerving for most men.

You will be worried and have to deal with fear, too, as you wait to learn what will play out. Unlike any other challenge in your life, these worries and fears will grip each part of your body and tense every muscle there. Then, as you become afraid, you may notice that your body is numb, weak or barely able to be used the way you need it to be.

As you wait to hear about your child, or wait to learn what has happened....or even wait to see what they are looking like for the first time, you will deal with all of these emotions, many of them all at one time. You will deal with anger and fear as well as pain and sorrow.

These are all normal emotions and you should be ready to face them, or so you may say to yourself. You will develop a coping mechanism to help you, which is normal to do. Then, when you have exhausted your thoughts and your tears defy you and roll down your face anyway, realize that it is normal and it is human.

Chapter 7

May 11th, Inside the ICU

And then, no matter what you have prepared for, it can't live up to what you see here, for the first time….

As I stepped through the doors of the ICU, I was overcome by this feeling of fear. I did not understand why, I just knew I was afraid.

I saw my daughter first. To this day, I will never forget that image that is forever imprinted in my memory. All of the visions I had tried to imagine to prepare myself could not even compare to what I was feeling. I wish I could put it into words. However, if you have been in my shoes, there is no need to try to describe that feeling.

I walked over to her bedside and took her hands into mine. I remember them being so cold with a tint of gray. She had tubes in her mouth, nose and ears. For the first time in my life, I saw a life support machine and it was hooked up to my daughter. It was providing the life that she was fighting so hard to save. I sat there for several minutes stroking her hand and face.

Then the chaplain walked me a few curtains down to my son.

Although he was not hooked to life support, he had tubes down his throat and a breathing tube around his nose. He was asleep from the anesthesia. I walked over to the side of his bed, gave him a kiss on his forehead, and whispered, "It's ok now. Daddy is here."

For about an hour, I paced back and forth between the two rooms. The doctor had come to see me and gave me the same news she had given me over the phone. The only good news was that my son was doing much better and was going to pull through.

Maci's chances were still very slim. The doctor informed me that they were injecting her about every half hour with "some medicine" in order to bring down her blood pressure. She pointed out the piece of equipment that monitored her blood pressure and told me the target numbers we needed to see.

I recall saying a prayer every time they injected her. I watched the numbers as they began to drop a little at a time. Then in a matter of seconds, they would start rising again, only to crush the little bit of hope I still held onto.

After I had been there for about an hour, the nurse came to Maci's room and told me my son was awake and was asking for me. I walked up to his bedside and his eyes were barely open. All I could think about was hoping he was not able to focus enough to see the tears flowing down my cheeks. When he saw that I was there he closed his eyes and went back to sleep. For the first time since the accident, he felt safe and secure.

The remainder of the night found me wearing a path between the rooms of my son and daughter. Every now and then, my son would open his eyes which would breathe new life into my heart.

Moments later, I would be reminded of the false hope as those dreadful numbers would fall – only to rise again. It was an emotional roller coaster I had not signed up for, and it appeared that I was the only one in line for the ride that night.

Chapter 8

In the Heat of the Moment

Any type of coping mechanism you planned to use was washed out the door as you entered the room and found your child there, needing you and wanting you to make it better, but there was nothing that you could actually do to save them.

During these tense moments, there is little to do but wait and hope and pray and wait even longer. There is little doubt that you want your child to pull through and make this all go away yet at the same time, you have no way of fixing it for them. You are afraid, simple and straightforward. Like it or not, just about every hard core man, with a steel body and a shielded heart will cry when they see their child like this. You love them, and therefore you are afraid for them and for yourself.

Being afraid right now does not, in any way, define your masculinity. Being afraid now is putting on the father hat and playing the role. It does not matter if the nurses see you crying. It does not matter if your hands are shaking and you cannot utter an intelligent word when you meet to talk with the doctor. It does not matter if you are trembling and hate the fact that you are so scared. All that matters right now is that the worst does not happen.

It is likely that you will beat yourself up, at least a bit, at the tears rolling down your face. After all, what man cries in situations like this? What you need to realize here is that most men cry in situations like this. It just happens and it's your emotional capacity that needs to come out and handle these terrifying minutes. Crying is acceptable and warranted here.

The Emotional Roller Coaster of Hope Dashed By Despair

As it happens, many situations are just like this one. Your child needs you and as you watch the numbers on their chart or on those machines move up and down, you try your best to force them there. You will them there. You devise a way to imagine they are going up even though they may not be.

When they do inch up, you convince yourself that this is it and this is the turning point that you had hoped for. Unfortunately, it is very likely that they will turn the other way and within minutes you are at the depth of despair that you hate to be at. It is very unnerving and painful to position yourself in such a situation.

In some ways, this emotional roller coaster can be more detrimental to your mental situation because of the ups and downs. In some situations, a straight forward answer is the best way to deal with the crisis. But, there is no way for that to happen here and you have to deal with it.

Many men will find themselves hurting and feeling incredibly alone in situations like these. Other men will feel themselves faced with incredible anger that there is nothing that they or anyone else can do. You may think to yourself that surely in this day and age there is something that can be done. You get frustrated when the machine's numbers won't change or when the doctor once again tells you that the treatments are not working. Why not?

As you go through periods like this, the length of time between emotions and interactions will cause your mood to change and it will likely cause you a lot of fear at the same time. It may help to bring out your true emotions as you force yourself through the process of dealing with each situation. Fear, anger, anxiety, terror...they all come to the surface in many ways.

This is often the situation in men when their children do not die quickly but rather the process takes time from days to weeks or even longer. They go through a period of "ups" when things look better and feel like they are getting stronger and period of "downs" where nothing but bad news is trickling in. In all situations, the ride is one you will never want to be on again and it is sure to create enemies and friends along the way.

As you wait and hope for something to go right, realize that there are others surrounding you that may be able to offer a bit of support and comfort, even to a man that wants to handle everything themselves.

Today, as you look back at the way that you handled these situations when your child was dying, take note of how you reacted and how you dealt with the ups and downs of this horrible roller coaster. If you are like most, you are not able to grasp the true pain you felt then in words. That is normal. It is also normal to experience all of these emotions as your child, your flesh and blood lies there.

Chapter 9

May 12th The Pivotal Day in My Life

The sun finally showed itself and yet Maci showed no progress.

The doctor brought me to a private room and I knew this could not be good. Without any hesitation or emotion, she informed me that they had done all they could and needed the family to approve removing Maci from life support.

I fell to my knees and once again wept uncontrollably.

It was a little after 9 AM when my ex-wife asked to see me. I entered the hospital she had been taken to and went straight to her room. I saw the intense amount of physical and emotional pain she was experiencing, and my heart went out to her.

Although we had been divorced for a couple of years, she was still the mother of my children and I will always care about her. I walked to her bedside and held her hand for several minutes as we both wept.

Shortly after arriving, a nurse walked into the room and told me someone had called from the Children's Hospital. Maci's heart rate had just spiked and they did not expect her to live much longer.

I rushed back over to the Children's Hospital and ran up to Maci's room. As I sat and held her little hand, at 10:08 AM, Maci went to be with God.

Surrounded by my family, I wept. That was the moment my world began to turn upside down and inside out. I could not even think about the decisions I would have to make in the upcoming days. Even more important than that, I was not sure how I was going to gather the strength to tell my son his sister was no longer with us.

I look back on that day, and the events of those 11 days afterwards are so fuzzy. There are so many details I cannot remember. There were so many people (I call them angels) who were instrumental in helping our family in those initial days, whether it was cooking food, visiting, or just being there to hold our hand. I will tell you more about some of those people later in the book.

For those of us who have lost a child, we will never forget that date and that moment in time. Everything we remember is referenced by that date. That is the day – the moment – when our world as we know it comes crashing down and we have to learn to start rebuilding our lives all over again.

During the funeral, the presiding minister made a comment I will never forget. He said, "When you lose a child, you never get over it, but you have to learn to get through it."

In these next chapters, I wish to give you an account of how I learned to live with the loss of my daughter. Don't think for a second that it is going to be easy. It's the hardest thing I have ever had to do.

I hope to open your eyes to the different stages of grief. Moreover, most importantly, I hope to convince you that it is ok to cry. After all, had I been using pen and paper to actually write this book, the pages would be stained with the tears that I have shed – tears that allow me to heal a little more each time.

A Moment in Time

I can't believe it's been two years
Since you left this world of mine.
It seems just like yesterday
I guess I've lost all concept of time.

Seven hundred and forty seven days
5 hours and 19 minutes ago.
I lost a moment in time
I can't get it back, this I know.

It was in that moment that you took your last breath
And your heart surrendered its last beat.
It was in that moment that my world fell apart
A blow that knocked me to my knees.

For in that moment, I felt the pain
As I sat by your bed and cried.
And in the moment, I let you go
As a piece of my heart died.

Some have said that a moment passes
As fast as you can blink an eye.
Others compare it to that distant star
A single twinkle in the sky.

So although the moment has come and gone
Every day it still lingers in my mind.
It is that moment I can never have back
That single moment in time.

I love you and miss you baby!
"Kisses and Hugs"
Daddy
May 2, 2003

Chapter 10

Your Spouse, Your Family

As life hits you smack in the head with this devastating loss, you are likely to face untold pain and suffering. Your situation is unlike any other, and no matter how much anyone tries to "understand", they simply cannot. No one will refute that feeling and it is your right to feel that way.

Yet, your child's mother may be someone that does feel the pain. While it may be unique to you, they too are likely suffering through something similar. For each situation, the test will be different. You may be married, divorced, or you may have no connection at all to the mother of your child. Your situation is different based on the way your marriage was before this happened and is likely different by the events that have happened since them, too.

It is important to take note that, if you do have a spouse, you can rely on them to share some of the grief and pain that you have. The mother of your child is likely experiencing their own levels of fear, terror, anxiety and depression. It may be easier to close the door to the bathroom, climb in the shower and scream until the pain goes away, or let the tears roll. But, crying together may be healing for both of you.

There is a particular book in which a very special section may help to showcase just how much grieving is an individual situation, and on that you are likely unable to share with even your spouse.

> *This grief, Theodore realized, was one of the few separating things in their life together. He couldn't help Suzannah here; he couldn't reach her. This particular part of her had died. If she had wept and grieved, he could have comforted her; the ground would have bloomed again. But, it was a sealed-over area no one could reach, where nothing would ever grow. He learned then about the isolation of grief, even for those in the same grief. Grief can't be shared. Every one carries it alone, his own burden, his own way.*

Anne Morrow Lindberg, *Dearly Beloved*

The same feelings experienced here are likely to be the ones you are feeling. You feel alone in your grief, and rightly so. Is there any way that someone could hurt as much as you do?

During your time of emotional instability such as right after the death of your child, you may experience several feelings. You may feel that you need to be the strength behind the scenes, handling the entire process of getting the funeral together and handling all of the sadness your spouse is experiencing. You may feel it is your duty to take care of her; after all, it was HER child. If you have family or friends with you, do not feel guilty about letting them take over some of those duties. They are grieving as well, but their pain is far less than what you are experiencing.

Yet, it is your child as well. And, when you come to think of it, you should be the one hurting and feeling the blow. Your child loved you, and you shared a unique bond with them. You may become hurt and angry that your child's mother is getting all of the sympathy in terms of pain when inside you are breaking just as badly, if not worse.

You may then become hardened to the pain. You can't possibly think about their death because it is up to you to keep the family together. You've heard the "statistics" that say that a marriage can easily end over the loss of a child. You know you have to keep it together, because someone has to, in order to keep your family's head above water.

All of these emotions are raw and they are likely to move through your body right after your child's death. Dealing with them is not easy, in fact, it is downright ridiculous. If you could, you would just shake everyone back to their senses to get on with life. But, then there are those moments, which just instantly melt your heart. For example, coming home from the funeral and trying to make it into bed only to step on those horrible Legos that are strewn through your bedroom that they left behind. In these moments, your heart melts all over again and now, you feel incredibly alone in your grief.

First off, realize that although some statistics do say that 70 percent of marriages end up in divorce, it is not necessarily true, or relevant. After all, you and your spouse have your own feelings and history together. There is no telling what your history holds for both of you. The only truth in the matter is that you are both here, having gone through a life changing event that will forever distort your relationship. You can work on rebuilding your new life together, or figure out how to do it alone. Take my advice. You do not want to go through this alone. If you find yourself alone, reach out to a friend who you can confide in and share your feelings. The life you save may just be your own. If you know of someone who is alone and has experienced the loss of a child, be that friend. Be the shoulder to cry on. You will make a difference just because you are there when they need someone the most.

Is It Possible to Share Grief?

As you go through your new life, because with your child gone, it is very much a different life than it was, you will see people in a different way. You may be angry at your spouse. You may be unable to communicate your feelings, which may push them away. You may not be able to "deal" with their tears and sorrow because it hurts too much to open those wounds.

There is no doubt in the fact that men and women grieve differently and that you and your spouse are going to have to find a way to get past all of these changes and challenges to cope with this new life.

It will be a challenge for you and your spouse to make it past these days, weeks and months. As you move through them, do realize that there is pain on both sides of the relationship and neither of you is going to get through this quickly or easily. It may be easier for you to try and grieve alone, but in effect, you will grieve together as your life changes, for the worse, in many situations.

Sharing your emotions can be helpful and healing, but as raw as you are from such a loss, it truly may not be possible either.

When Decisions Have to Be Made

Take a step back for a moment and consider the way that you and your spouse need to work together during this trying time. For example, if you and your spouse had to make the decision to remove a child from life support, it is heart wrenching and utterly impossible to do. This may be made worse when you both do not agree on the correct way to move.

Another example is with organ transplant. In many cases, doctors only have a very short amount of time to ask you both to make this decision. You may not share the same opinion as your spouse.

Still, later, there is no doubt going to be conflict in terms of making decisions about burial or cremation, location and the funeral. You both may not share the same views on how these things should be handled. It may be quite complex for each of you to make such a decision on your own, and you should not. Still, together you may not be able to communicate enough to make a good decision.

When you find yourself in a situation like this, where there is an important decision to be made and you and your spouse cannot seem to agree, take a step back. Your feelings and emotions are important, as are theirs. What is important to see here is that a decision should be made for your child's benefit. Finding a way to communicate during these periods can be very difficult, but it will need to be done with a level head on your shoulders.

Communication at this point is more important than emotions, even though the decisions you make will be based on your feelings for your child, their mother and the entire situation. Still, coming to a decision together may be forced and you may never be comfortable with it. Making it together will help to overcome some of the difficulty that lies there, though.

Sharing Your Loss with Family

Perhaps nothing is worse than losing your child, but it is never easy to actually have to say the words to those that you know and love. Telling them that he or she is gone is painful, heart wrenching and it will definitely stir every emotion that you have pushed aside and away.

For some men, this is the breaking point. For example, having to tell your son that his sister did not make it can be the worst punch in the stomach. You'll hate it and you will hate it even more that your emotions betray you when you know you need to be strong for someone else. While difficult, seeing you cry and expressing your feelings may be good for them, too.

There are no easy ways to say what you have to say and even if there were, no father that loves their child could make it through those words without crying. It is normal, it is expected and it is necessary.

Crying with others when you share this information may be difficult for you, as it would be for anyone. Yet, it may also help you to express the true depth of the situation to that person.

As you stand here today and look back at the way that you told of your loss to those that ask, you may wonder how you did it at all. It may feel unlikely to be words that actually left your lips. It may pain you incredibly to hear the questions that will come including "Why?"

When telling someone about your child's death, it is normal to feel as if your heart is being ripped out of your chest all over again. Whether you realize it or not, though, this is part of the grieving and acceptance process. You will make it through that pain.

Chapter 11

Stages of Grief

You have heard it before. Grief goes through stages. You go through stages of how you are dealing with each point in your life.

When you think of grief's stages, do not think of the stages as a straight line. Rather, think of them as a continuous line that moves back and forth all the time. You can even think of them like the pendulum of a clock.

What is difficult is knowing that grief changes, but sometimes when you feel as if you are moving forward, you may find yourself falling back, into the pain that is nearly always there.

In this chapter, we talk about the stages of grief. I'll examine my own stages of grief then include information about the actual "textbook" versions and why they happen. My story is true and by no means have I mastered grief.

What Is Grief?

Grief is a word that is used often and often too lightly. Unless you have lost someone that is very close to you, such as your child, grief may not truly define the feeling correctly. Sadness does nothing to define the way you feel, nor does heartache, as it is often referred to, far too lightly.

Grief is a situation in which your body, your mind and your soul are profoundly torn and near destruction. Grief rocks your body physically, emotionally, and mentally. Grief is intense, perhaps the most intense feeling you have ever felt in your lifetime. It is an overwhelming situation that leaves you without control. Grief is also confusing as no one understands the "why" or the "how" questions that it asks. Grief is frightening as you try to cope with the thoughts and feelings of moving on, moving forward or just moving in general. Grief is the dark unknowing, not sharing any hope for tomorrow that you feel as if you cannot move past today. Putting it plain and simple, grief will change your life. Grief sucks!

No one knows how to handle grief until it hits them. No one understands the pain that another feels even if they have been in grief themselves. There is no training and no preparation for this time of your life. Perhaps it is best that there is no training and preparation because this type of pain is singular and far too intense to go through more than one time.

Understanding the Stages

In Elisabeth Kübler-Ross' book titled, *On Death and Dying*, she introduces the discrete stages of grief that have been known to become "The Five Stages of Grief." According to Kübler-Ross, the stages are denial, anger, bargaining, depression, and acceptance.

Although some people I have talked to have not gone through all of these stages, there are others who experience every stage. I am one of those "others" who not only visited each stage, but went through a couple of the stages more than once.

After about six months of losing Maci, I started attending a group called The Compassionate Friends (TCF). This is a support group for bereaved parents who have lost a child. Attending this group was the best thing I could have ever done. It was nice to be able to open up and share how I was feeling through each stage of the grief process without being judged. As a matter of fact, just the opposite happened. I learned that many people in the group were experiencing or had experienced the feelings I was fighting with on a daily basis.

One of the first things I learned from my new group of friends is that grief is like the pendulum of a clock. In those early stages of my grief, I just assumed they were like speed bumps in the road. As I got over one speed bump, I would be ready for the next one. That was not the case at all. Not only can you experience more than one stage simultaneously, but just when you think you have gone through a particular stage of grief and ready for the next, the pendulum swings back and forces you to revisit a stage you had previously gone through. Grief sucks!

Why Is It So Complex?

It would be easier if you could just move from one stage of grief to the next without having to look back. Unfortunately, along the way, there are going to be things that happen that cause you to fall back. An anniversary, a toy or even just someone asking the dreaded question of "How many children do you have?" The key is to keep your eyes and heart moving forward.

You may never get over the loss of your child but you can learn to adapt to it. Even the term acceptance may sound impossible to you at this point, but you can lean to construct your life in such a way as you can move from point A to point B and even live a happy life. It just will take time and a number of detours to get from one place to the next.

One last fact that is important to know is that you may not necessarily go through the stages in sequential order. I will say it again...grief sucks!

First, you may be angry, then bargain, and then actually deny the entire fact. Once you hear the news, you may bargain with God, deny it, and then become angry.

As I walk you through the next five steps of grief in this book, I wish to simply define the stages of grief, share with you my thoughts and emotions as I traversed these stages, and how I continue to battle to overcome them.

Denial: This Simply Cannot Be Happening

When it comes to defense mechanisms, this is the first one that slapped me in the face. The thought of losing a child was just too painful to accept.

The denial process for me started with the phone call. "Someone is playing a sick joke on me." "They must be mistaken."

"It must be someone else's family." "I just talked to my kids a couple of hours ago. There is no way it could be them."

I tried and tried to reason in my mind that this was not happening. I have often heard stories of father's who were awakened in the middle of the night by a phone call or a knock on the door to only hang up the phone or close the door in the police officer's face. "There is no possible way that is my child. He is staying at a friend's house tonight. You must have the wrong person."

The one thing that I experienced and most fathers who have lost a child experience is that the denial stage is the shortest lived stage of grief. Many men I have spoken to do not even experience the denial stage. They immediately put on their game face and begin being the pillar of strength. However, like many other men, I went through the denial stage. Although it was short lived, when the facts are brutally in front of you, it is difficult for men to further deny the facts.

When I saw my daughter in the hospital bed, I was in denial that she would lose her life.

When the doctor told me they had done all they could do, I was in denial.

When they took her off the life support, the denial stage was over. For me, it lasted about 15 hours.

For me, it was the least difficult stage of my grief because I still had a gleam of hope – as little as that gleam may have been.

So, for me, there was not a certain point in the denial stage where I personally did anything to take me to the next stage. On that same note, I never went back through that stage again. I think for us men, once we get through the denial stage, we never face that particular animal again.

Why Do We Deny It?

Denying what is happening is a normal crisis mode reaction. When we deny what is happening we allow our brain to digest what was just put in front of us.

In *Life After Loss,* by Vamik Volkan, the author writes appropriately, "Denial is a shock absorber that helps us slowly absorb the truth."

This is true and perhaps the best way to explain the way that you are feeling. Denial is not harmful to you, as long as you work through it. In some cases, it may take some encouragement and it may take a gut wrenching scream to actually let those feelings out. Denial is your minds way of working towards the understanding of something that is so difficult to grasp. For each person, this stage will take on a different form and of course a different length of time.

Nevertheless, it is this realization that there is nothing that you can do, say or believe other than the fact that your child is gone that will launch you into the next stage of your grief.

Anger's Crushing Blow

Anger is one of the most basic emotions. This is a stage of grief that was very difficult for me.

Initially, I was extremely angry with the man who drove onto the interstate the wrong way, and hit the car head on. Later, when I heard the details of this man's life, how he suffered from mental illness, and how he expressed remorse in the court room, it was difficult to be angry with him.

I certainly could not be angry with my ex-wife. When I saw the news reports and the pictures in the paper, it was obvious that she did everything she could to avoid the collision. Had she not acted the way she did, it could have been much worse.

So, who was I going to be angry with? The most common answer to that question is God.

I became extremely angry with God. How could he let this happen to me? Why did my seven year old daughter have to die? What did she ever do that was so bad to take her life?

I turned my back on God. I did not want to have anything to do with him. There were times that I even questioned his existence. This is when my life started going downhill.

In the time that I really needed God the most, I blamed him and was angry with him. I turned to the bottle and tried to drink my problems away. (During these times, I also went through the bargaining stage.)

Thinking about maintaining a relationship was impossible. I shoved anyone and everyone out of my life. The anger was just eating away at my heart. Before long, my relationship was non-existent, I had lost my job and my home, and I had made poor decisions that I will live with for the rest of my life.

It took me three years to finally leave the anger stage for good. Although I had still been attending the monthly Compassionate Friends meetings, it was not enough to pull me though this stage. It took me hitting the bottom and having no place to go but up, before I started my slow exodus out of the anger stage.

I started to pray again. After all, God knew what is like to lose a child. Reading the Bible became a daily ritual for me. I began writing more poems which seemed to be a healing release for me. And after three long years of harboring and battling these feelings of anger, I was free.

Do I still get angry from time to time? You better believe it. Some of that anger raised its ugly head as I wrote this book. But I continue to ask God to forgive me and help me take it one day at a time. You may not feel that God is the answer to your current situation, but he was the answer to mine. My only regret is that I did not let him back into my life sooner.

When Anger Bears Its Ugly Head

For many individuals, anger is the stage of grief that is most difficult to deal with in terms of day to day life. Anger is a situation in which there is no resolution. No one can say anything to make you feel better. No one can help you to see that it is okay. It is up to you to work through your anger at your own pace, step by step, until the entire process has been resolved by your mind and your heart.

Anger shows itself in many ways. You may feel angry at your lost child for leaving you, even if there was no way for them to control what had happened to them. A parent of a child that is older, perhaps one that is caring for the parent, can feel abandoned. It is particularly common for parents who have lost children to drug overdose or suicide to become angry with the child for doing this to them. How could they do this? Some parents even become angry with their child's friends. How could they not have seen the signs? Did they see the signs and just choose to ignore them? What kind of friend would do that?

It is very painful to be this angry and in many situations, that anger is directed at those in your life that you feel you can be angry with. Sometimes, it is directed at anyone who is close enough to have to take the blow. Sometimes that is a spouse other times it is God. In all cases, you get angry with others because in some way, shape or form, someone has to take the responsibility for this.

You may come to a point where you feel the need to hold someone or something responsible. There is an undeniable need to explain what has happened. Even though there is no real explanation available, you need and want to have some-one to hold accountable.

In some situations there is a real accountability that can be placed on the person. For example, if a drunk driver is respon-sible for the accident that killed your child, you definitely have someone specific to blame. This can easily allow anger to turn into rage. You may become enraged by the people that allowed them to drive in the first place and then enraged that they did not get enough of a sentence in court.

Anger is not a one shot deal. In most cases, it can lie in wait and will come out at any time. You may find yourself irritable and impatient. You may find yourself with a short fuse most of the time. Although you may not be angry at that moment in time about the death of your child, the anger from the death has not subsided.

For some, there is an irritability that leads to frenzy. For example, you may find yourself completely capable of moving through the steps of choosing a coffin and planning the funeral. Almost like a business deal, you work through the process without a problem. You seem strong, willing and capable. This is not necessarily an acceptance of what has happened, but a way of dealing with the frustration and anger you are feeling.

Each person has their own way of dealing with and expressing their anger. In each situation, you will need to take note of that anger or the feelings that are similar to it. Knowing that this is what is behind your anger is an important part of moving on to the next stage.

Forgive and forget, yeah right! Forgiveness plays a huge role in ridding yourself of anger. However, we will never forget. It's just part of our human nature. The sooner you can start to forgive, the sooner you will see the anger spells diminish. However, this is certainly much easier said than done.

Bargaining

Bargaining is a negotiation between two parties. In the grief process, I found that I was bargaining with God. This was another stage that I visited on more than one occasion.

Once again, the bargaining started with the initial phone call. After hanging up, driving to the airport, the entire flight, the drive to the hospital, and through the next morning I bargained with God. "God, please let my children live and I will do whatever you ask."

I remember being in The Gulf War and on many late nights and early mornings when I was on guard duty, I would pray that God would let me make it home safely to my wife and son. I bargained with God at that point in time in my life as well. I found myself having the same conversations with him that night. I was not in a combat zone, but my children were. They were fighting for their lives.

This was another stage that did not last very long – about 15 hours. What else was there to bargain for? God was punishing me for something I had done (so I thought at the time). Do you see the pattern yet? Now I was back in the stages of anger.

It was in those long nights where I sat on my back porch with a bottle of whiskey in one hand and a picture of Maci in the other that I did my best bargaining. I was no longer bargaining for my children's lives – I was bargaining for mine. In a drunken stupor, I would pray that God would let me sleep. When I did sleep and had those dreams of Maci, I prayed that God would keep me awake. Once again I bargained with God. "God, if you will please get me though this, I will be a better servant." It was in this time that I suffered depression to its fullest.

Bargaining for a Hope

Bargaining with God or with any other aspect of your life, even yourself, plays a role in the grief process for most people. Begging for a chance to change what has happened was important. It can also be important later on when you find yourself without a way of getting through the depression and anger you feel.

Bargaining is your mind trying to bargain with itself. When you bargain, you are trading something that you find appropriate for something that you need such as acceptance or peace.

For some people, the bargaining process also encompasses the level of guilt you have. If you wish that you had told them not to go out that night that they were hit or you may feel guilty about the fact you did not realize they were doing drugs. Bargaining here may be a way of allowing yourself to cope with these feels of dread and pain, of being the one that caused this to happen. You may have no direct responsibility to the situation, but you feel as if you do.

Bargaining may be your best way to gain hope. There is no easy way to work through these feelings, but you likely will work through them quickly. Bargaining is a way that you will come to the realization that nothing can be changed, and that only you can help yourself back up onto your feet.

Depression

The simple definition of depression is the downturn in one's emotional state.

In my case, I was diagnosed with situational depression – an emotional state that arises from a particular event or cause. This is the stage of grief that I lived the most. I felt like I had a monopoly on depression. I never thought that I would be happy again and be able to enjoy the things I used to enjoy prior to Maci's passing. I never thought that I would be in a normal relationship again where I would not constantly fear anyone that got close to me. I thought that this dark cloud of depression would follow me everywhere I went. I did a very good job of disguising it though.

I can't tell you how disgusted I would get when someone would say, "You are so strong. I do not know what I would do if I ever lost a child." They would have the same choices that the rest of us have.

Choice number one – we learn to live with the loss.

Choice number two – we take the cowardly way out and take our own lives.

I chose number one. Don't get me wrong though. Often times when I was bargaining with God, I asked that he take me out of this world. I thought in my mind that was the only way I could ever be free of the agonizing pain I was living with.

I look back now and think how selfish I was. I have parents that would experience the same things I was experiencing and I would not wish that on my worst enemy. More importantly, I have a son who needed his dad. As I look back over the years though, I realized that it was I who needed my son just as much as he needed me.

The drinking just caused the depression to become deeper and deeper. To get through the day, I threw myself into my job. At nights, I was drinking myself to sleep.

Eventually, I went to a doctor who prescribed me medication to "take the edge off." This was more of a mistake than the drinking. While on this medication, I never cried or showed any emotion. I did not care about anything at all.

It was during this time, that I made mistakes in my life that I will always regret. Although I was numb, I did not realize I was just temporarily burying the anger and sadness. Yes, I eventually hurdled those mistakes and am a better person because of it. But, it was a long and sometimes seemed like a never-ending road. Depression is normally your first sign that you are beginning to accept reality. Depression sucks!

Depression Can Change Your Life

Depression is a real health concern. The fact is; it is a life threatening condition in many ways. If you or someone you know is suffering from depression, and has had suicidal thoughts, it is important to seek out professional help. Yes, working through depression is an important part of the process of dealing with the grief of losing your child. Yet, when you put yourself in a position that is so low that there is no way out, professional help may be necessary.

Depression is also a time for realization. Here, you are no longer grappling with the idea of losing your child. It has happened. It hurts and there is no answer for it. You may feel that you no longer have the strength to be mad at the situation. You may also feel that there is nothing more to look forward to.

Many people that go through a stage of depression will hit rock bottom. Not only are they emotionally drained, but there can be a physical toll as well. Men are prone to face health problems. Many of these health problems center around stress related problems.

Stress affects people uniquely. For some, it may cause ulcers, for others it leads to alcohol and drug abuse which can lead to acute health problems. Smoking more than ever is common. Many people find themselves unable to sleep and have to face insomnia for some time.

Depression takes a toll on the body because of stress in general. You may be unable to do the things that you used to do. You may also find yourself facing daily aches and pains that seem to come from nowhere.

Yet another part of depression is the feeling of being mean-ingless. What reason do you have to get up in the morning? Why should you go to work and bother with people when there is no point? After all, even though you loved your child so much they were taken from you?

Another way that people express themselves is just the oppo-site. You may be the type of person that drowns themselves in their work. They tell themselves they have to work to protect and provide for their families. They spend most of their day, and even their night working, completely unable to do anything else. In many ways, this meaningless feeling is one that can prolong depression.

It will take some time before you can move from being in this depressive state that consumes your life into a more productive or healing state. For each person the length of time will be different. The way that you deal with depression will be different, too. It will take a long time for you to work through this stage as you come to grips with the tension, the pain and the agony of what you feel.

Whether you mask it or you face it head on, depression is the most serious and most detrimental part of the healing process. Yet, you are working towards healing when you are here. But still, depression sucks!

Acceptance

I cannot put a finger on the moment I accepted the fact that Maci was gone. I cannot even tell you the timeframe in which it happened. It just seemed like one day I woke up and I felt as if everything was going to be ok. Things actually stopped "sucking" so badly.

I can tell you that I had stopped the heavy drinking and ceased the prescribed medications. I truly visited and revisited the different stages of the grieving process.

But don't think for a minute you are home free. Do not be disillusioned by the fact that you are entering the final stage of grief. Remember, grief is like a pendulum of a clock – you go back and forth. As I previously touched on, acceptance goes hand in hand with depression. It is truly when you start accepting the loss of your child; you will probably experience huge waves of depression.

I still go through emotional states of sadness. I call it sadness rather than depression because it is short lived. It is normal though. Here are some times that I experience those short-lived times of sadness.

The anniversary of the loss is one of those times. As crazy as this is going to sound, it is true on most accounts. The anticipation of the anniversary is normally worse than the actual day itself. After all, as you are going through the stages of grief, it is impossible to think that one day can be worse than the next.

Try to reflect on the good times and reward yourself. As unhappy and depressed as you may feel, you will be able to look back one day and say it was a stepping stone in the walk of healing.

The birthday of the child is another instance. This was always a very difficult day for me, but I always make sure we celebrate it. Some people will think you are crazy. Others will think you need to let it go and move on. Who cares what they think? This is your game and your rules.

The sixth year of Maci's passing was the first time I did not get a phone call from someone in my family to see how I was doing. Did I notice the phone did not ring? Absolutely. Did it bother me? Absolutely not. It just served as a reminder that a parent never stops grieving for his child no matter how much time passes.

However, we still make a chocolate cake and eat peanut butter and jelly sandwiches. Those were Maci's favorite, and happen to be mine as well. Call me crazy if you want. I don't care and neither should you. After all, this is your child and you do whatever makes you happy. There are no rules when it comes to grieving.

Holidays will always hurt. The first few holidays (especially Christmas) were the toughest. However, we still make Maci a part of our traditions. We light a pink candle in memory of her. We hang the stocking and place one pink rose in it. We have an ornament made for her every year, and we continue to decorate the tree with the ornaments she made. It is now a tradition to go to the mall and pick an angel from the tree and buy gifts for a less fortunate seven year old girl. I am certain that Maci smiles when she sees us honoring another child in her name.

Graduations are difficult. I try not to spend a lot of time dwelling on the graduation. Although I was several years into my grief before I attended a graduation, it still hit a spot in my heart. Knowing Maci would never get the opportunity to experience graduation was hard for me. However, I now try to focus on the graduates, as it is their day.

One thing we have started is a scholarship to a boy and a girl in which all of the profits of this book will be contributed to.

Weddings are one of the worse events. Weddings are still very difficult for me and will be for every father who has especially lost a daughter. When I see the father walking the daughter down the aisle and giving her away, I feel a huge pain in my heart.

Although as fathers we never really want to give our daughter away, we know how special that is to them and we long to share that dream with them. After all, it is one of the most honorable events in our lives that we share with our daughter. Walking our daughter down the aisle is one thing in this huge glamorous ceremony that is reserved for us dads alone (that and the father-daughter dance).

So yes, these events and many others will always remind you of the things you will not be able to do with your child that is now with God. However, the important thing is to remember that you will always have these feelings of short-lived sadness.

It is not a setback – it is merely another step in the healing process.

You don't get over it but you do get through it.

Acceptance? Is that Possible?

Depending on which stage of grief you are currently in, you may be sitting there wondering if you will ever be able to actually accept what has happened. After all, how can any-one ever be okay with such a terrible loss? The fact is, you will need to accept what has happened. And, although you will never forget, you can move forward one small step at a time.

Another way to look at acceptance is to think of it as adapting. During the entire process of grieving, you are working to pull yourself from the way you feel and force yourself into this new situation. During the process of grief, you will learn how to learn how to deal with the loss. You will learn how to handle your emotions. You will need to resolve the issues and scenarios that are holding you back. When you accomplish these goals, you work yourself towards acceptance.

As you work through these things, you are slowly letting go of the bonds that hold you to your child. After time, those bonds will weaken and you will find new ways to fill in where they left off, even if it does not feel like that is possible right now.

You will always have your child as part of your life. You will find that one day it will feel okay to put the toys away or to finally give away their clothing to someone that can use them. One day you will see that you can let go of any bond that holds them to you, so that you can move forward.

Take your time with acceptance and learn from it. Never allow anyone to push you into letting go. For some people, it will take much longer than for others. There is no due date on this project, no expiration date on your love. One day, you will just feel as if the weight has lifted enough for you to move on.

By no means does this mean that your child has to leave your life for good. In fact, it is just the opposite. When you enter acceptance, you position yourself to do more for them than before. You'll be able to look for ways to honor them and you will feel comfortable talking about them again.

Complexities Exist that Can Worsen Your Grief

Each person deals with what has happened in their own way. Sometimes there are outside causes of additional grief and pain, though. These complexities are often hidden or may not be evident until it becomes very poisonous to their emotional state.

A good way to see this is as a foundation. For some, the foundation is much stronger than for others. As the problems roll in, all the foundations are shaken, but only those buildings on a weaker foundation will fall. Some people simply can handle more than others do. If you cannot handle the shaking, then you may collapse painfully. When you lose a child, these things can come out in full force even though they were never problems before now.

There are three main situations that are causes for concern but are commonly seen in those people that do not have as strong of a foundation to start with. Long standing problems such as mental illness, substance abuse problems and personality problems can easily come to the surface during situations where you are faced with your child's loss.

Mental illness can become pronounced especially in situations where people find themselves to blame for what has happened. You were driving the car that was in the accident that killed your child. You were not watching them close enough when they ran into the street. In situations like these, guilt can overtake someone that has a shaky foundation to start with, causing them to continuously, long term blame themselves for what has happened.

Sometimes, mental illness is never even considered. People may simply believe it is just guilt. Yet, underneath it all, it may very well be guilt that is brought on by manic depressive disorders.

Personality disorders can also be an underlying problem that the loss of your child brings to the surface to the point where they must be dealt with.

For example, a child may become involved with alcohol but the father who would never believe the extent of the problem with his perfect son, never allowed for that child to receive the necessary help he needed. Not only that, but he was in complete denial of any problem that the child had. In effect, he caused the child's death because he did not provide the emotional and physical protection the child needed through consoling. Because of his ego and attitude towards his perfect son, he never got the child help. Thus, the child was lost and the father remains in a depressive state that is all consuming. How could this happen to his perfect son?

Substance abuse is another common situation for those that are faced with the loss of their child. If there is any weakness in your foundation here, it is likely to come to the surface with such a devastating loss. What is important to remember is that alcohol or drug use, both prescription and illegal, are ways to mask the pain. At first, that may be the reason that you use it.

Yet, when the substance abuse becomes necessary to keep you going, the problem is much deeper. Some people are more likely to abuse alcohol than others are. Some are able to stop after they work through their anger and move on.

Others will continue to struggle with this problem, now brought to the surface for some time.

Ask yourself where you are in these stages. Do you find yourself in a place of anger and rage? Are you still asking God to take you instead? Understand that these are normal feelings that any man will have as they deal with the loss of their child. In the long term, the child's loss will always remain. What does not have to remain is the pain that you feel over that loss.

Chapter 12

Men and Grieving

Men and women grieve in their own way. The reason behind this is actually very simple. Men and women are raised in different ways, believing different ideals about the way that they should react to situations emotionally.

Society portrays women as the ones that need to be cared for and the ones most likely to reach out to other people. Men are taught to keep their feelings to themselves because it shows weakness. Men are taught to keep their hearts hidden where women are encouraged to talk and to show all of their emotions.

Women are more likely to develop emotional and physiological problems. Many believe this is due to the fact that women are more likely to visit the therapist while men are more likely to do anything they can to avoid doing so.

Even though this may be true, both men and women share the same feelings, underneath it all, about grieving and death. The way they express that grief is what makes women and men so unique and completely opposite in the grief world.

Men should be strong and handle problems based on fact alone. Women are encouraged to handle struggles through emotions. Women are more able and more willing to get in touch with the way that they feel. In turn, women are more likely to talk about the way that it feels to lose a child, while men are more likely to tuck that emotion away and never deal with it.

Women are more expressive in their feelings about death and loss and therefore seem more likely to be in distress. Yet, just because you do not express your pain and fears does not mean they do not exist. It would be the same as saying microorganisms do not live in your kitchen because you do not see them there. They are there; they are just hidden.

That is not to say that this scenario cannot be flipped in the opposite direction. In the majority of cases, men are more prone to hiding feelings and not dealing with them while women instead spend their time working through those feelings. In some situations, men are the ones that are more willing to express their feelings and more likely, then, to get help for their grief. Women may be the more silent and reserved type, not willing to deal with their feelings.

Nevertheless, in most relationships, there is one person that is more expressive while the other is less likely to convey these thoughts out loud. Determine where you are in this scenario. Which role are you more likely to play in your day to day life, regardless of the grief that you feel? Has the grief you feel so confounded the way that you would be "normally" that now you find yourself expressing your feelings all the time, whereas you may not have done this in the past?

These situations are very normal when dealing with such profound loss. The underlying connection remains the same, though. You need to express your feelings, learn to get a hold of them and learn how to deal with them so that you can move through your day successfully. By doing this, you are not forgetting your child or making their death less painful or less important. What you are doing is seeing a light that only tomorrow holds for you, personally.

In many situations, it may seem as if the mother of the child is getting more attention and focus from others around them. While most men would never admit that they were in the least jealous of this, your feelings may be hurt or upset that you do not get the same attention as the mother. Why is this?

For some people, the fact that the child spends so much time with the mother means that the child has a better connection with the child, right? Many people believe, mistakenly, that a mother grieves more for a child than a father can. After all, they held the child in their womb for 40 long weeks and they spent all those long days playing with them at the park.

Although this may seem to be the case, spending time with someone like this does not mean that they should grieve more or less. It does mean that the person in this situation, mother or father, will face more daily reminders of their loss.

For example, if a mother stayed home with her child for the first five years of life, and lost the child to a horrible accident years later, there will be instant reminders of their time together throughout the house. Sitting on the couch watching the news may allow your hand to run over a stain on the fabric from when the child spilt something. Daily habits are different because the child is not there to care for.

In this way, the instant and constant reminders of the child can cause more emotion to come up and be on the top of the mind. Nevertheless, dads do go through the same types of situations, perhaps not as often. (Of course, the situations could be flipped here if dad spent more time with the child than mom, did!)

The Expression of Grief

Perhaps the most important thing for men to realize, and for mothers to also take note of, is the fact that although a man may not show that he is suffering from the death of his child, he is. Whether by choice or by necessity he does not show his emotions although they are on his mind, in his heart and part of his life each and every day.

In some relationships, after a child dies there is talk and argument over this very thing. "Don't you care that she died?" "Why don't you cry, don't you miss him?" These words are often misplaced on men because, although they have the same underlying feelings of grief, they do not express it in the same manner.

Sometimes it comes in other forms. When a friend approaches and tells you that they are so proud of how strong you are and how you are holding it together for everyone, they may not be giving a compliment after all. Inside, many men are facing an internal struggle about this very thing. They know they are barely holding on and to them, not doing so is a failure.

Because they do not understand the way that you grieve does not make them bad. Nor does it make you bad if you do not express your feelings in the same way they do. What needs to happen is an understanding and an agreement that everyone will suffer in their own way. Love is not in question here, only the amount of expression that is being shown.

Dad's the Hero

Another way in which men grieve differently has to do with the average role that they play. In many families, children look up to their fathers as the heroes. They are the ones that you go to when something is wrong and you don't want mom to flip out. They are the ones to help you learn to hold a bat the right way. They are the ones that will show up at the playground ready to defend their child who is facing a bully. Dad is the hero.

This can add another layer of grief to the father. After all, in not being there and not saving the day and "allowing" the child to die, did you not fail your responsibility of being the hero?

These emotions can weigh hard on any man, including those that struggle from day to day with hiding emotions. The feeling of letting the child down can even worsen when they begin to allow things to fall apart, at least somewhat. Not only are they letting down their child, who is now gone, but they are letting down their family by not being the pillar of strength they believe they need to be.

You are her hero. You are his hero. You are the one that shared the most important times of their lives with them. You saved the day many times. And, although you couldn't save the day that final time, it was beyond your control, much like the tornado that rips through a town or the hurricane that comes barreling at a city to level it. It is out of your control even though that barreling and that ripping of your heart will forever cause you to change.

Why Men Just Don't Cry

What many people mistake a lack of emotion for is the lack of crying. Most men do not cry or at least do not cry in public, where others can see that they are suffering. This is a normal reaction with men based on what society has taught them over time.

Men often deal with their grief in other ways. For example, some men go back to work within days of their child's funeral. Men are more likely to go play a game of golf within months of their child's death. Men are more likely to stop after work with friends to get a drink. They do this not because they are avoiding their emotions, but this is their way of crying.

Men share the same emotions as women do but instead of tears flowing down their face, they instead put their mind to work. They go to their job and they use it as a distraction. They use it as a tool to getting back to normal. Sometimes, they go out with their friends to get away from the pain they see throughout the home they shared with their child. Other times, they go out with their friends to feel as if they can be near to something normal and do something that they "should" be doing.

Instead of crying men sometimes get angry. As mentioned earlier in this book, men and women go through anger as part of their grief process. Yet, sometimes, that anger can be put aside with a cold beer or a shot of liquor. Are these things the right thing to do when you are grieving? Nothing that will hurt your body or put at risk is, but many men feel the need to use these as coping methods, such as crying works for many women to get through the pain they feel.

Grief Avoidance

There are some situations in which men will try and push the grief from their minds, hoping without hope that it just goes away. They do not want to feel the pain of not having their child to spend their lives with. They do not want to feel the lack of control that they have.

To deal with grief, they work their hearts out. In other situations, men will work to put grief aside by focusing on something else. If they tackle another problem, perhaps one that is less emotional, they do not have to deal with those emotions.

When you do try and avoid grief, you do not necessarily overcome it. The grief does not get better, nor does it go away forever. It may be something you do not have to think about for a few days, perhaps longer. Yet, it comes back and because you did not think of it before, it may be more painful to deal with later.

Avoiding grief is not coping with grief. Avoiding grief will not take away the pain, either. It may draw a huge line in the sand between you and your spouse. It may cause your life to shatter around you even though you are trying to hold it together. Should you grieve even though every part of you does not want to? Doing so is the only way to move on with life and put this pain to rest at least somewhat.

Crying in Silence

While tears may not stream down your face, and you may not have the ability to grab hold of your wife and pour your heart out to her, realize that crying can happen in other ways.

You may cry in silence, feeling the hand of pain gripping your heart and squeezing. Though tears do not fall from your eyes, you feel as if they do. You may cry in silence by giving up the things you love because you feel as if you do not deserve those things any longer. Men cry, in this way, because of the loss they feel but often because they could not control the situation.

In other situations, crying feels right and should be something you allow to happen. If you visit a religious organization and pour your heart out to a priest, you may be concealed enough to feel safe in expressing emotion, but you may be able to understand a bit more.

Other times, like at night on your child's birthday or on Father's Day, you may very well want to cry your eyes out. Instead of finding something else that is more important to do, allow the tears to flow. It is in these times that healing can take place.

Chapter 13

How Mourning Is Shaped and Structured

Mourning is a word that draws sadness from anyone. The word alone feels cold and sorrowful. Each person mourns, in their unique way, facing their true being. It is important to understand that the way that you mourn is based on your unique personality, your history and what your beliefs are. There are no wrong answers, only ones felt from the depth of your heart.

Your personality determines how you mourn and in most cases, when the day comes to mourn you have little control over the way that you feel. You do fully control the actions that you take in terms of what you allow yourself to feel and what you do because of those feelings. Yet, what causes those feelings if very much a factor of your personality.

There are several concrete things that affect the way that mourning is structured for most people:

- The type of personality you have defines it
- The type of relationship that you have with the child, defines it
- The previous experience you have had with death and loss, defines it

- The circumstances of your life which are and are not in your control
- The people around you effect the way that you mourn

With so many things causing your mourning to be one thing or the other, how can you actually achieve success in terms of getting over these feelings?

There is no easy way to answer that question, though there are many ways that you could. In this chapter, I aim to discover what shapes your mourning, as a man that has lost his daughter or son. By fully understanding these concerns, you may be able to shape your grief in a better way.

Personality Factors Define Mourning

There are various factors of your personality that will play a contributing role in the way that you grieve. These factors, which range widely from one person to the next, are things that are part of you. For example, if you were to ask your best friend to define your personality, they may say, "He's hardworking and responsible." "He's aggressive and goes after what he wants." Just as these small sayings can define who you are, so can the personality factors that determine how you will grieve.

Guilt and Self Blame

One personality trait that can complicate the grief you suffer is that of self-blame and guilt. If you are prone to feel guilty about the death of your child, it is likely that you spend at least some of your time wondering, "What did I do wrong?"

People that suffer in this way do not get past the phase of "What could I have done to stop this from happening?" They likely do not feel the loss in the same way, because they are destroyed by the fact that they did something to cause it to happen in the first place. Instead of moving from guilt, to loss, and into a state of pain and then resolve, they remain in the phase of self-blame.

Many in this situation feel profound loneliness in their grief that is unexplained by their situation. That loneliness often translates into not questioning their feelings against what others think and therefore never learning that they are not to blame. In these situations, you may not ask for the support you need.

Extreme Denial

Another personality trait that can cause an individual to suffer more severely is extreme levels of denial. For most people, the denial stage of grieving lasts only minutes, perhaps hours. Realization sets in that this has happened and must be dealt with now. With others, this is not the case. They know in their mind that the child is gone, but they try to perpetuate the situation as long as possible.

For example, some people may put off telling loved ones that the child has passed. They may even decide to simply cremate the individual, have no memorial service and go on with life. For men, this can happen easily as they drown themselves in work, never allowing themselves to actually think about what has happened.

Extreme denial may not be as evident as you may think. People may go through the motions of life without thinking about the fact that their child is gone. Rather than remembering her when they sit down for a meal, they are completely consumed in other things that they do not allow themselves to acknowledge that it happened.

Control

Men are more likely than anyone else to feel the pain of their daughter or son's death as a loss of control. You may feel powerless, out of control, or unable to grasp what is happening because it seems to be something beyond your control.

The level of control that a person has is often determined by the way that they perceive control. For example, if something were to happen to you, do you blame the person that made the problem happen or do you blame yourself for being in the wrong place? If you were to be walking down the street and someone ran into you, would you blame them for not paying attention? Would you blame yourself for not paying attention? The perceived control you have often defines what type of mourning your will suffer form.

If you are the type of person to blame others, you may become obsessed with who is to blame for your child's death. In cases of accidents, it can be hard to forgive and we are not implying you need to (though it can highly beneficial later on.) Do you accept that it was an accident or do you continuously go after the person because they did this to your child?

If you are the person on the other side, more likely to blame yourself, you may be unable to give yourself any room and any ability to believe that the situation is not your fault. You may, for example, take self-blame to a level that causes you pain and keeps you from actually moving on from your loss.

Previous Emotional State

Another factor that will shape your mourning is your ability to grieve based on your emotional state before the death of your child. For those that are in a good position prior, with a good amount of control and a good self-esteem, it is more likely that you will have a better time healing than those without this.

For example, if you had a good marriage, were a fairly stable person and low key, low anxiety and had a good outlook on life prior to your child's death, you are more likely to have an easier time working through the grief. While you will suffer, you are emotionally stable prior to the incident, giving more ability to overcome the situation.

For those that start out with emotional instability, it is likely that grieving for a child will be much more complicated and painful. In most situations, those that expressed a level of high anxiety or emotional turmoil prior to the death of their child will suffer longer through the grieving process. They face a more complicated grieving process because of this emotional instability.

Relationship with the Child

How does your relationship with the child matter in terms of the way that you grieve? Are there factors that cause one person to grieve more than another? Is it harder to grieve for a younger child compared to grieving for an adult child?

There is no way to say that one person grieves more or that the grieving process is the worst if you lose your precious baby instead of your 35 year old son. What is important here is that these grieving processes are different, unique to themselves. Your relationship with the child is what defines the depth of grief you need to deal with.

Various areas can make that death more difficult to handle. In a younger child, parents are more likely to be with the child more often. They tuck them in at night and they get them out of bed and to school in the morning. They feed them, they scold them, and they play with them. At a younger age, there is more day-to-day interaction with the child, which can compound the grieving process of the death of this younger child.

Additionally, grief can be made more complicated by situations in which the child is in. Should a child be a teenager who has been causing a lot of turmoil in the family, their death is no easier. Yet, it is different. The relationship has changed and the interactions are different. In some situations, these relationships can be even more complicated as the parent may feel as if they did not do enough to keep the child out of harm's way.

The amount of daily interaction with the child is a key factor in the complication of grief. Another area that can change the grief is when a parent has a strong emotional attachment to that child. While most parents will not admit it, some children are easier to emotionally become attached to. In these situations, parents can put in a place where the child's loss is profoundly difficult more so than in other situations.

The relationship that you share with your child will define the overall grief process to a point. Adult children, new-borns, even miscarriages are still deaths of children. It is important to consider, then, that the loss is always profound, yet in some cases, it may be more complicated.

Life Situations Alter Mourning

Your life is completely different than that of your neighbor. If the same tragedy struck two families at the same time, it is likely that they would mourn in different ways. The reason is quite simple. Your life situations at the time of your child's death will play a role and effect the overall complication of your mourning.

One of the most prominent things that will define your mourning is the stability of your marriage or relationship with your child's mother. If you were divorced or married, there is still the level of quality that was found in that marriage. If the marriage suffered from turmoil prior to the death of the child, it is likely that it will suffer even more so now.

While speaking of marriage, several things will define the likelihood of your marriage surviving. At the time of your child's death, you may cling to your spouse for support, in your own way. As time passes, things change. Some people blame their wife for not being there to protect the child, after all, isn't that why she stayed at home? Others will feel as if they let their spouse down and cannot handle the self-guilt that they feel in doing so.

There are several key things that must happen during the mourning process for a marriage to survive. The level at which you both can accomplish these things will determine what the end result is.

First, the couple must allow each other to mourn, in their own way, at their own pace. You may be ready to go back to work after a few weeks. Your wife may need more time to work through that same level of grief. Realize that the mourning process will be different from one person to the next and that there is nothing wrong with this. Do not be demanding or critical of the other person. This will not in any way help your grief or theirs.

It is also just as important that you respect your partner's grief. If your wife is ready to go out with her friends for a drink, realize that this may be acceptable, especially when your wife is in need of the companionship. On the other hand, if you want her to go out and get back to the things you both enjoy doing, do not force it. If she is not ready to do so, allow her the respect to make that decision.

Finally, it may also be important to consider intimacy. Some people will seek out intimacy as a way of being close and releasing the tension that they feel. Others will fall back into themselves, unable to share this type of bond. Be respectful of your partners needs in this regard. Each should be able to be respectful of the others needs here.

Stresses and Supports in Your Life

If there are stress factors in your life, the mourning process will be more difficult than it would be without them. There are many situations, which can make the process of grieving even more difficult. Things like financial strain, divorce and problems at work simply complicate the process more. They put more emotional and physical strain on you. Sometimes it can become too much.

The mourning process is partially defined by the level of stress within your life. The more complicated daily life is, the more difficult it will be to cope with the emotional loss of your child. There is little doubt that this will leave a large scare deeper than any other turmoil you may be in. Yet often, it is these additional stresses that break the camel's back.

Just as you have a number of added stress problems that can affect the level of mourning you endure, it is also likely that there will be a number of supports that you may have that can "lessen" the pain. Again, here the goal is not to say you feel less pain, but that you may have a different mourning style. You may cope better if you have a stronger support group around you.

Support comes from all sides, the family, friends, even from coworkers. Having a strong support group is essential to working through grief. If you are not someone that has a lot of support, it is likely that you will have a more difficult time working through your grief.

I did not have much support in my life, at least not in close proximity to me. My entire family lived across the country and I had few close friends to speak of. My support system however was always a phone call away at any hour of the day. However, I chose to push anyone and everyone away from me. I completely shut them out and tried to control this myself. Yes, it is a man thing, but something I soon learned to overcome.

Not having support readily available to you is not an excuse not to get it. While that may seem like a harsh statement to make, the fact is that it takes support and other people help push many through grief.

There are many outstanding support options out there, some of which will be mentioned later in this book. The key is to remember that there is support available to those that need it and do not readily have it available to them during their grief at home. You may even want to seek out support in other forms from strangers, as it may be easier to talk about the way you feel to them. Regardless, what is important is that you strive to have support that will help you by under-standing your grief.

Each of the topics discussed in this chapter are a piece to the definition that defines your level, depth or complication of mourning. You may or may not find yourself in these posi-tions. Nevertheless, it is essential to realize that there are many reasons why you could be having a difficult time work-ing through your grief.

Chapter 14

The Nature of Death Does
Define Mourning

The way in which your child died does play a role in the way that you grieve for them. Men often take a unique approach to the situation in comparison to women. Yet, in both situations, especially in traumatic situations, the cause of the death will weigh heavily on the way you mourn.

As you work through your grief, take a step back and see your anger, sadness and fear for what is behind it. Are you angry at the doctors that did not save your child? Are you angry at yourself for not noticing their problem before it was too late? Understanding the way you feel about the problem is an important part of recovery. In some ways, you may be able to take the way you feel and change the outcome for other parents such as through helping with medical research or by helping to educate people about drunk driving.

Here is a look at several types of death commonly found in the deaths of children. Notice how each type of death is different from the next. While no one's grief is more or less than the others, it is important to realize that the grief is different in its own way because of the circumstances surrounding your child's death.

Sudden Death

Sudden death is one of the most difficult of all types of death. If you lost your child through a car accident or in other ways suddenly, you are dealt one of the worst possible blows. Not only is it very difficult for you to come to terms with the death because of its depth, but it will likely be more complicated to get through.

Unlike the death of a child through an illness where it may take longer for the child to die and therefore gives the individual more time to mentally prepare for this situation, you do not have that luxury. Instead, there are no more "I love you" to say to your daughter. No more high fives to give to your son before they are taken from you. You do not have the ability to say goodbye, which, though difficult, is one of the most important aspects of moving forward through grief.

Shock, overwhelming disbelief and inability to finish business with the child are some of the most difficult parts of this way of dying. Because the death is so complicated and so unreal, your ability to cope with it has been greatly reduced. There is little chance that you will find yourself able to work through the grief until the shock wears off. Despair is much deeper because there is no time to prepare.

Unlike with an anticipated death, the death of your child simply does not make sense. How could this really have happened? It does not make sense to any part of your being. In a longer illness, for example, there is time for your mind to grasp the fact that the child is ill and therefore, there is something that makes sense behind the loss.

In sudden death, there is no time to get ready. There is no time to think about the "what if" situation or if they will die. Instead it is thrust upon you and you just have to handle it.

Many times, it will take time to learn how to cope with this sudden death. You may need time to leave things the way they are. Many parents do not want their child's bedroom to be moved or touched, as in their subconscious they are not ready to accept the situation as real. Allowing this to happen can help you to step through the death slowly, until you come face to face with it in your own way and your own time.

It is important to note, though, that while sudden death of a child can be more complex, in long term study, there is no difference in the parent's recoveries afterwards. In other words, both anticipatory and sudden death grief can be coped with successfully.

Complications and Added Circumstances

There are many types of sudden death that can extract even more emotion from you.

Murder

For example, if your child was murdered, chances are good that there are many feelings raging in you. Many men feel extreme anger in situations like this. There are two aspects that seem to make this even more complex. One, parents often face the fact that their child had to suffer before they died. They may have been in pain and hurt. This is heart wrenching for most parents to cope with.

Secondly, because murder is voluntary, the simple fact that the death was intentional fuels pain and rage for many men. They often find themselves facing a no-hearted legal system that provides plea deals to those that killed their child. They are often faced with long, drawn out attention from media, police officers and ultimately from the court proceedings. Then, when the ruling comes, it always feels the same, "Is that all my child's life is worth?"

Suicide

Another area in which parents often suffer incredibly is through suicide. When a child takes his own life, the world has changed in terms of grief. There are a new set of emotions and society factors to face. Most men are likely to be intensely upset about the death of their child in this manner, particularly if they did not have any type of indications of problems.

For most parents who are facing the death of their child from suicide, there is an unreal sense of pain to face here. Most will ask the same questions about the situation of themselves.

- Why did this happen?
- Am I an unfit parent?
- Didn't they love me enough to stay?
- Didn't I do enough to make them happy enough to stay?
- Why did I allow them to go through life like this?
- Why did you beat his confidence down?
- How did I not see the signs?

Society is often the most difficult in parents of children who die in this manner. Many parents force these societal ways on themselves, though. They often believe that society sees them as bad parents that were failures that did not do what was needed to raise their child. While in some cases this may be the reaction, in most it is not. In many situations, society simply does not know how to react and talk to parents in this situation.

There are other situations that also contain these same scenarios. Children that die from drug abuse or from AIDS will leave their parents in similar situations. Many parents feel that society looks down on them for allowing their children to do drugs or not getting them the help they need. AIDS is still an area fueled by hate and it too comes with a stigma.

Many people whose children die from drugs and AIDS also face another emotional toll. They often feel that society does not care about their children as much as others. For example, if a child is doing drugs, drinking and can't hold a job, that child may be seen as more trouble than value. This in turn can elicit a lot of pain for families as well as anger. Is my son not as good because he has an addiction?

When dealing with mourning, there is no black and white. The way that you feel is defined at least in part by the way that your child died. While it may not be something you can grasp right now, in all situations, men have the ability to work through these emotions and position themselves to work through grief. It is never easy in any type of death, but you can go on living.

Chapter 15

A Further Look at the Stages of Grief and Moving Past Them

Earlier in this book, I talked about the stages of grief. I briefly went through them, examining the way that I felt as I trudged through this time of my life. I mentioned that I still struggle with some of those stages, as you will throughout your lifetime.

It pays to take a closer look at these stages because, as I learned, they played a significant role in the days, months and years after your child's death. In this chapter, we explore the stages more fully, so that you can take this information and apply it to your life.

Additionally, we will talk about how you will move from one stage to the next. Remember, there is no way to do this yourself. Instead, you will need to move through these things as your mind and emotions allow you. Nevertheless, it is important to realize you will move through them.

Denial

Denial is the first stage of mourning. For many people, denial is a fast lived stage. For others, it starts long before the child dies, such as in the case of a child dying from an illness. In all cases, denial is your body's way for absorbing the shocking news you have just been told.

Denial is a tool, a defense of sorts that allows people to put up a shield and to stop the pain from reaching them. In some situations, denial can be a physical symptom. Some people claim that the instant they heard that their child was taken from them, they felt their heart rip apart. Some describe they feel as the heart dropping out of their chest.

Men will deal with denial in many ways. Some will simply not acknowledge the problem at all. "What do you mean she's dead? You are being ridiculous?" Others deal with denial well, as well as men do by hiding the emotion that comes to their face. Some fight, some flee.

In other cases, denial is a situation that allows a person to cling to hope. Even though in most cases, denial is a very short lived stage, there is still the hope that this is just a mistake. It simply cannot be true.

In denial, some people can show no outward expression of that feeling. As we mentioned earlier, the mind thoroughly understands that the child is no longer with them. Yet, some-how they believe that if they go through the stages of their day not paying any attention to the situation, they can simply deny that it every happened.

These situations can be very real to men who bury themselves in their work and lives not facing the pain and sorrow that they feel. They know their child is no longer there, but they do not actually acknowledge this fact, never talking about it with anyone and avoiding the conversation. Much like the child that hides by covering their face, if they don't face the child's death, then it didn't happen.

Take a second to consider why you deal with denial. Have you moved on from this stage? Can you accept the fact that your child is gone? Even if it truly burns at the pit of your stomach, facing the fact that it has happened is the only way to move from this stage on to the next. It takes a huge amount of courage, but it is a giant step that brings you that much closer to healing.

From one stage to the next, that is the only way to pull yourself through the next few months or longer.

Anger

Anger is a very powerful emotion and one that you will not likely leave behind as quickly as denial. You are angry at the situation. You are angry at the people that did not save your child. You are angry at your spouse, the neighbor, the person that dares get in your way right now!

As raw as anger is, it is also a powerful tool in moving you forward. When you are angry, you will also be accepting what has happened. In order for you to be angry, you have to have something, like the death of your child, to be angry about.

Men may express this emotion better than any other. Many men lose control at least sometimes through rage or through words. Often, it is at the expense of those around them. Expressing your anger is a good thing because it gives you the power to move forward and soon you will.

Think about the level of angry that you feel right now. Are you angry at someone? Are you angry at your child for leaving you? Or, perhaps you are angry about the circumstances that have caused you to be going through this? All of this is natural. Next, consider how you are dealing with that angry. Are you expressing it in some form through either words or actions? Are you boiling inside? Are you able to release it n your own way?

In order to move forward, you need to expel the angry from your body. You will never walk away from it fully, but you can lessen the blow it is having on your body. Many times, it takes an explosion of emotion to take you on to the next stage of grief. You may be able to facilitate this by driving the anger from you. How can you do something like this? One way is to find an activity that you enjoy and that gives you power and allow it to work for you. Buy a punching bag and use that to work out the angry. Go to the batting cages and take your anger out on those balls flying at you. Go out back and chop some wood. Take a long hard run. Do anything healthy to dispel the anger.

Take notice of the way you are showing your anger to your family. Are you saying things you regret? Realize this and learn to stop your tongue. Are you hurting others physically? Are you short tempered, easily annoyed by those around you? If so, these are all expressions of anger that are deeply rooted in the loss of your child, even if they seemingly have nothing to do with your child.

Take notice of your anger. It sucks being angry all the time. Provide yourself with an outlet to let it out, finally.

Religion and Anger

Many people go through their anger in its own stages. From blaming yourself to being angry with those around you and often being angry with God, this normal path will likely have you staring your religion in the face.

Many people position themselves to be angry with God because God is easy to blame. For those that believe, God has control over this situation. How did He let this happen? How could He allow a child to go through what your child went through? Why is He doing this to you?

It is natural to blame God for the problems in life. When larger problems such as your child's death happen, the amount of anger that you have can be incredibly fierce. There is no tangible person or object you can blame for your child's death so you direct your anger at the God that is supposed to be looking out for your child. It makes sense, but it can lead to a completely new experience down the road.

For some, being angry with God is only the start. Many will turn from God, through blame and in some cases hate. When there are no answers forthcoming, anger can turn from blame to hate. In many situations, the result is a turn from God for good. Some people walk away from God not believing that a loving and caring God could do something so cruel. Others, position themselves to blame God and therefore be unwilling to trust in him.

When a turn from God happens, the people who attended church each week may stop. They may instead turn from him to other substances. These evils can easily enter your life and transform the way you think and see your future, your child's life and even God himself.

Even though this pain is so intense, many people will turn from being angry with God to being ashamed in the way they had lead their lives, again blaming themselves for the death of their child. Men often do this in terms of being the protector and the one that lost control.

As you struggle through your religious beliefs in why this has happened and what you have done wrong to fail God, take a good look at your situation. Step back and let go of the anger enough to see what is truly happening. As with any stage of grief, you cannot move past one onto the other through a decision to do so. However, you can find relief.

Start by turning back to religion, if you do believe and have made this part of your life now. Talk to a priest or another individual in the organization that you feel comfortable talking to for your situation. Privately, share your thoughts about why this has happened and how you can move past your anger and pain towards God.

Analyze for yourself what religion can offer to you. Can it provide you with a welcoming embrace? Perhaps you will not understand why God would do this, but perhaps you can find the way to trust in Him again. Knowing that this is part of His master plan or that your angel is now in his loving care, may help to ease the anger.

Turning back to religion is not an easy step, especially for men that may not have taken an active role in religion prior to the death of their child. Turning back may help you to grow closer to God and acceptance of your child's death. Anger may rage, but it will lessen when you move from where you are back towards love.

Anger is not a stage that will completely be gone from your life. While denial may never be something you come back to, anger may linger and come out when you least expect it to. Some days, such as your child's birthday, the anger will come to the surface all over again. It may happen several days before, even. You may not consciously realize that your irritability and anger are actually a cause of the birthday. Most do not make the decision to be mad. It simply happens. Yes, I know. It sucks.

Working through anger is essential. For those that do not, and tuck it in their stone cold wall of no emotions, the pain can be increasingly real. If you do not expel anger, you will live with it and allow it to change whom you are and what you stand for. Find a way to allow it to leave your body so that you can move from anger towards acceptance.

Bargaining

A bargain is a deal. In a sales transaction, you bargain for the lower cost. You bargain to get a better product. You make a promise to provide more for an improved result. In bargaining with your child's death, you are trying to make a deal with God.

Bargaining is a cold place to be, one that is looking for a bit more hope. Can you bargain to save your child's life as he is suffering from an incurable illness; is there any possible way that you can trade your life for theirs? A bargaining process is a good step towards the right end of acceptance. When you move towards bargaining, you are moving more towards realizing that there is no opportunity to get back what has been lost.

Later, through depression, many bargain with God or with their life because of alcohol or drugs. You ask for the pain to go away and may even give up on life because of this. If stopping the pain means dying, then so be it, is a common feeling. No, this feeling is not right, but it can be understood.

Bargaining then changes to a stage where all you can do and want to do is to work through the pain. If it just stops, if you can just forget, if you can just move on...you will do anything. Most men do not verbalize these feelings, but they suffer internally with them. Some think about it, others simply push them aside. Anger can come through bargaining, too, often because there is no bargain to make.

The realization of that, that there is no bargain to be had, is one of the most profound movements forward. Nothing will change the loss of your child. Nothing you do today will take away the pain that you feel. While the pain will not go away, the pain will improve and over time, you will learn acceptance.

Bargain with God, with your body, with your own spirit. Bargain with the devil and that bottle of alcohol sitting on the table or the drugs you know you can get. Bargain with your job and your coworkers, daring them to come in your way. Bargain with your spouse who is likely doing her own bargaining with God.

No matter how many bargains you make, promising empty or full, you will find yourself standing in the same place you are in right now: with no benefits, with little change and with a life that you could live in a better way.

With bargaining comes a bit more of acceptance. The realization that only you can make the change is real and it is powerful. Next, take the most important step you can take and work towards accepting that nothing can change your child's death.

Depression

Before you can get to acceptance, you must go through depression, in most cases. Not all people will get to the point of being fully depressed, but as we talked about earlier, each person deals with grieving in their own way.

Perhaps you can understand the pain of depression clearer when you have gone through the loss of a child. Depression is a time of profound pain, much more than being sad. You feel the pain in each move you make during the day.

Depression in men is very different than it is in women. Women will express their depression in obvious ways. They will be more willing to display their feelings so that others can see. Some women, especially those that need the physical and emotional connections to get through depression, will verbally express depression in words, actions as well as in day-to-day activities.

Men go through depression in other ways. Men often will try to cover up their feelings, even as raw and as horrible as they feel. Most will not say that they are depressed. They will not be willing to say they are depressed. They also are likely to deny it both to those around them and to themselves. They are not depressed.

Being depressed is for weaker men. Being depressed is unacceptable and is a problem only women go through. These are very real sentiments that many men express. Yet, most men, yes, most men, will suffer through some stage of depression throughout their lives, especially evident in the death of a child.

Society plays a role in the way that men express depression. Men are often seen as weak or less able if they show that they are depressed. While this may be the view of many, it is necessary to realize that you are in depression, or that you will go through depression at some point in the healing process.

Life will not be normal again. You will never feel the touch of your daughter's hand caressing your face. You will never get to tell your son how to hold a football the right way. You will never view your family, your other children and your friends in the same light. It will always hurt to think about your child, though in a different way. You cannot fix it – you cannot control it.

All of these feelings are likely to come to the surface as you go through depression. Yet, it is in these actual feelings that healing can start. Everyone will go through a different level of depression. You will need to hit bottom before you can pull through the pile of pain you face. However, depression is the vehicle to getting towards acceptance.

You will not feel normal again. You will not feel the same way you did before your child died ever again. Your child's mother will never understand the profound change in you. Perhaps the only people who will understand are the other men you meet that have also gone through this loss. Even then, life will never be the same and that feeling is what you need to deal with.

Life will not feel normal, but it will be acceptable at some time. You may never get to laugh at your child's incredibly funny opinion on the clothes men wear in football games or the way that they seem to find the most bizarre comments to make. Yet, you will laugh again. In fact, these memories can help you to build that happiness in their memory. Most in depression do not realize that there is a way out, though, not yet, not until you have hit rock bottom. I don't have to say it but I will…it sucks.

Depression often leads to dependency on alcohol, drugs or other addictions. Because you are vulnerable, you are more likely to go to the bottle for a bit of healing. It is essential to monitor this move as you could allow the accident that took your child's life to also take your own.

Many men will need to seek counseling and help for depression. There is little doubt that this process will be easy to do, but it will open the door for opportunities in healing. You will find a time during this stage where you are willing to do anything to get back to life or at least to stop the pain. In that time, work towards acceptance by seeking out the help of professionals.

Later, we talk about organizations that can help you to accomplish this goal. For right now, realize that there are others out there that do understand the way you feel and that want to help you. Talking to someone does not have to be a chore, if you allow yourself to open up enough to let them in. If you cannot talk to your loved ones, find a professional that you have no stake in and can open your mind to. Allow them to listen even as you express your feelings of depression.

Depression is self-consuming and it often helps to realize that this very personal battle is one that you can overcome. Like the other stages of grief, you cannot force yourself to be over depression. It takes time and commitment to get through it. You can find a number of ways to get through this a bit easier, though.

- Counseling: While many men will not want to do this, it can be one of the most helpful ways to understand and work through depression, especially when you find someone you are related to.

- Support Groups: Unbelievably, there are other people going through what you are right now. They have lost a child and the men in them understand the same pressures you are under. Support groups can help you to find a connection with others that also understand.

- Friends and Family: Not everyone has someone that they can connect with far enough away from the situation to help them. If you have a close friend or someone that you look up to that knows you and understands your grief, they too can help you to overcome the situation.

Depression can go too far, too. It is essential that you realize thoughts of suicide or self-inflicting pain are not acceptable and they should never be a part of your life. If you get to the point of not wanting to live and the thought of taking your own life enters your mind, then you need to seek professional help. Many of us reach the point in our grief where living is just an option we can take or leave. This is a natural part of the process – and one thing you probably won't hear at the office of a professional therapist. However, you will hear it on the lips of those survivors who have lived through the loss of a child. Saying "not wanting to live" and "taking your own life" are two completely different battles. If your pain is so intense that you feel you must take your own life, then allow someone to help you move through this very low level of grief. It truly does not have to be this way.

For those that are suffering from depression, no words on this page will help them to get through it without first understanding that you do not have to be depressed. Your life does not have to be consumed by grief and pain. The fact is you will find much of your life specifically revolves around this pain. You may think no one understands and no one can reach out to you. This is your own unique suffering and no one can take it from you.

For those that are scared to move on, too hurt to see through the dark shadows of depression, or unwilling to realize that around the corner is acceptance, realize that time can help. Allow yourself to move through depression at your own pace. Move on only when you feel you can.

Once you have been able to move through depression, and you will, you will begin to grasp acceptance. When you are ready to explore acceptance, you will need to take that step back and look at your life. Make some key decisions like these:

- Do I want to live like this?
- Can I overcome this?
- Am I worth the work it will take to get from point A to point B?
- Is the memory of my child worth living for?
- Do I have something to offer to others that may help me through my grief, too?

Examine your situation, closely. Realize that with life, there is no easy road to healing, but acceptance is a way of living your life around your pain. You will get there, one-step at a time and one day at a time.

Acceptance

Acceptance is not being okay with your child's death. Acceptance is not writing off the pain that you feel. Rather, acceptance is an understanding that you have with yourself that your child is not here. Life must move forward and, although you are never going to be okay with it, your child simply will not be part of life in the same way.

Everything will be okay. You will find solace in your life in some form. For most, there is no one moment that you will just wake up and say, "I accept that my son died and today I will go on." Instead, often the reality that life just goes on no matter what has happened helps you to move from one place to the next. In other words, life moves on, with or without you, and you likely will be part of that movement.

As you work through the stages of grief, realize this is an outcome that is going to happen. You will learn how to live your life successfully without your child in it. You will be able to breathe in and out, to get up and go to work, to meet the guys after work, to spend time with your wife, to start and finish a round of golf….to do all the things that you would have done. It will not be a simple move or change, but you will learn and your heart will accept the loss.

There will be times when you feel the loss of your child all over again as if it was just yesterday. You will relive the memories that you are trying so hard to push back right now. Birthdays and anniversaries are likely to be the worst part of the package. Yet, you will likely find yourself able to go through them.

One day, your child's birthday will come. You will know because there is no way you will forget. You will look at pictures and you will be sad for your loss and longing for the touch of their skin just one more time. Instead of spending the day in your room, crying, or fighting with whoever dares to get in your way, you will smile instead knowing that God is with your angel and that they are safe there. Then you can sit down and enjoy a peanut butter and jelly sandwich without the crust. That's what I do because that is what Maci would have wanted.

For those that can and are willing, there is peace in knowing that they do not have to suffer through the world's pain. Instead, God saw it right to take them early. In addition, perhaps the pain you feel in the loss of your child not so much as wronging them, but rather a loss for yourself. This world was not good enough for your child because God had the promise of wings already waiting for your son or daughter. They were perfect already.

Acceptance will come to you and when it does, you will make it through the day, the week and the years with more peace than you can imagine.

What's My Opinion on Greif's Stages?

One of the things I learned at The Compassionate Friends is that men and women grieve differently. I believe there are several different reasons to our differences in grieving. Although my beliefs are neither medically nor scientifically proven, the credibility lies in the number of men and women I have met who have experienced the loss of a child.

I believe one of the main differences men grieve differently than women is because of the relationship we have with our children. I believe women are more connected on an emotional level with their child. When a child is physically or emotionally hurt, more often than not the child turns to the mother.

The father's role is to be the provider and the protector in the family. We as fathers feel it is our responsibility to provide a solid foundation for our families and ensuring the necessities of life are provided.

The father is the pillar of strength – the superman that defeats the adversaries. He is the one who checks underneath the bed to ensure the "boogey man" is not there. The father does not cry when hurt, physically or emotionally. Moreover, as a father, no matter your stature, your child believes and boasts that you can beat up the other kids' fathers.

Another main difference is society driven. Growing up, I was taught that boys did not cry. As a father, I taught my son the same things. As a soldier for 12 years and a combat veteran, I was too tough to cry. Society looks at crying as a sign of weakness. We are expected by society to be strong and to be that pillar of strength for our wives and other children. In addition, do not even think about taking off work to try to work through your emotions. Take the three days of bereavement and be ready to get back in the saddle after the funeral. When out in public as a couple, the mothers are asked how they are doing, while the fathers are ignored. That is society and it will probably never change. In turn, as fathers, we will probably continue to grieve the "society-accepted" ways.

The important thing to remember about grief is that it is normal, but more importantly, necessary. It is part of the healing process. The timetable for grief is different for everyone. I tried to bottle up my feelings and emotions. I turned to alcohol and prescription drugs. I made mistake after mistake, until it finally caught up with me. Eventually, you will grieve. The sooner you start grieving, the sooner you can start to try to get on with your life.

For those of you who are new in your bereavement, you do not see any hope in sight. Although it is a long hard road, I assure you that there is life after the loss of a child. What you have to find out on your own, is what is going to get you through each stage of the grieving process.

One last fact that is important to know is that you may not necessarily go through the stages in sequential order. First you may be angry, then bargain, and then actually deny the entire fact. Once you hear the news, you may bargain with God, deny it, and then become angry. As I walk you through my journey of grief, I wish to simply define the stages of grief, share with you my thoughts and emotions as I traversed these stages, and how I continue to battle to overcome them.

I once heard someone compare grief to a heavy backpack. I remember my days in the military when we would go on road marches with heavy backpacks (we called them "rucks."). I recall the first couple of marches being almost unbearable. I could not believe they would ask us to carry so much weight on our backs. However, as time passed and we did more road marches, our body became better conditioned and the weight did not seem to be so heavy after all.

The comparison between grief and backpacks makes perfect sense to me. Imagine your backpack of grief being so heavy that you do not think you can take a single step. You use every ounce of strength to taker that first step. Then you take a second step. You realize that after some time, you begin to actually cope a little more. Your body is becoming conditioned to the grief. Before you know it, the backpack seems lighter even though you did not remove the grief. Before long, it will just become a part of who you are and this "new life" after your loss.

As fathers, we will always grieve differently than the mother. One person expressed it as "suffering in silence." I prefer to call it "shedding the silent tear."

The Silent Tear

What is the silent tear you ask
And how does it leave its mark?
It is that tear that nobody sees
Leaving its trail inside my heart.

Everyone asks me how I'm doing
And I reply, "I'm doing fine."
I force a smile upon my face
Each and every time.
And then I shed a silent tear.

I still have many days
When I am all alone.
I let the tears fall down my face
Wishing you were not gone.
And I shed a silent tear.

I thought I heard your voice the other day
As I was driving down the street.
I heard you whisper, "Daddy"
And my heart gave into defeat.
And I shed a silent tear.

It's the silent tears that hurt the most
Because they're locked up inside.
The tears that fall so freely from my face
Have no place to hide.
But still, I shed a silent tear.

Everyone around me goes on
Living their normal daily lives.
Not knowing my heart is broken
And that a piece of me has died.
And I shed a silent tear.

So baby when you look down on me
Each and every day of the year
Just know my heart is weeping
And I am shedding a silent tear.

I love you and miss you baby!
"Kisses and Hugs"
Daddy
March 01, 2002

Chapter 16

Coping with the Rest of Your Life

Today, no matter where you are in the stages of your grief, is the first day to start coping with the rest of your life. We could say "living life" but what you are doing right now is living your life, just not in the way that you could be. Grief leaves us raw and painfully aware of just how little time we have on this planet and how limited out time with those we love is.

Today you learn to cope. Life is not as it used to be. It does not matter if your child passes away when he was 20 or when he was two. Life is different today than it ever was, and, that is okay. You will face many troubling weeks and months of grasping at acceptance, but once you do, you next need to face the many ways that your life has been altered.

Look at the death of your child as a devastating hurricane that comes on shore and forever changes the landscape. Parents never really get back to a normal world. Instead, they enter a world that is forever changed in the way it looks. Instead of trying to get back what you have lost and working towards having the same life, integrate the loss into your new life.

Your life will change after the death of your child in several ways. Here, we look at several of those so that we can carefully outline the full extent of what you can expect.

Loss of Innocence

As the pain begins to pass and as time moves through the shadows of night and the rays of the day, there will be a loss of innocence that you feel. There will always be that dull ache in the pit of your stomach. Your life will never be as perfect and clearly outlined as it was before your child's death. Now, the perfect landscape is cluttered and broken everywhere you look.

If you were innocent, or not struggling through grief, you would see death as something that happens in the distant future. You are able to live day by day as others do, with no real thought of death and dying. Those who have gone through this kind of loss experience the loss of this innocence. Now, you see death as something that could happen at any time. As devastating as that sounds, most that face complications from grief and deep grief will no longer see death in the same light. It is something to think about and is something that can instantly change the way you live.

It is also difficult to move through life in the same way. No longer are you happy for the bride and groom getting married, or at least not in the same way. A sense of jealousy and longing that your child could share in this experience will be there. Christmas will be different because they are not there to rip open their gifts. The thrill of Easter egg hunts for the younger children will be different. Passing out candy at

Halloween will be a chore instead of a thrill. Mother's Day and Father's Day will take on a brand new meaning.

No longer is the paper black and white, because now there are many things to think about in between the lines.

Value Changes

Nearly all parents that have gone through the loss of their child will find that it is nearly necessary that they find a way to offer something to others that are suffering. I chose to write this book. Men and women both gravitate towards others that understand their pain. You may do this through support groups or in other ways. The key thing to remember is that this bonding is a healing force that many simply need to have in their lives.

Many will use this experience to help others too. If you have lost a child, you feel compelled to find ways to help others that are suffering through the same thing you are. Helping others that are also struggling especially newly in their grief is a gratifying way to spend your time.

Others turn their pain into good for the cause. Mothers and fathers team up to help work on cures for disease and now have a better dedication to helping in ways that their child lost. For example, if a drunken driver killed your child, you may find gratification in working to tighten laws and educating others. If your child died from cancer, you may want to work on fund raising to help others avoid such situations.

Another way that your views and priorities will change is through a heightened sense of awareness of those around you who are also struggling with death. For example, many fathers can see through the walls that other fathers put up when they too are faced with an illness or death of their child. You may not have been able to see the value of adding this to their lives had it not been for the death of their child. Now, individuals seek ways to offer help.

In the same way, you may become more sensitive and compassionate to those around you, especially in terms of death. Another value that is seen that changes is the simple way that success is defined.

One of the ways men in particular change after the death of a child is their definition of success. Many find that striving to work 60 hours a week and seeing their families very little is not as important. Instead, they tend to want to spend more time with their loved ones than they ever did.

What difference does it make if you are financially set and at the top of your company if you cannot spend time with your family? They want to see their children grow up and experience retirement early with their loved ones.

You Are Empowered

You are empowered. Depending on where you are in the path of grief, you will one day make it through to acceptance. When you do, you will have won a long and hard fought fight. You stood in the line of one of the most difficult circumstances out there. You survived perhaps one of the most wrenching types of pain ever experienced by anyone. In addition, you made it.

You may not want to get stronger, to get through to this point, but you did. You somehow managed, or will manage. When you do, you will be empowered because of your experience. This will only happen after you have broken free from the hold of grief.

You will appreciate life more now that you see how easily it can be taken from you. While the battle is not easy, the fact that you have reached a place where you can appreciate life is a bit of peace. You may be empowered never to take things for granted again. You may be empowered to do the things that you never thought that you would do but always wanted to. You will see the value in living life to its fullest because, if you do not, you are not living the best way you can.

What option do you have? When you are faced with your child's death, you really only have three options.

1. You can roll over and die, literally or figuratively.
2. You can let it drive you mad.
3. You can accept it and move on with your life.

As you move through grief, you are likely to face these hard choices often, but in the end, most will find a way to accept what has happened and move on with life to the best level they can.

Defining Death Now

In the loss of your child, you came face to face with death. Its ugly head destroyed your life and for that, you may be hurting to a level that you simply cannot handle.

Still, now that you have seen death in its rawest form and felt its hand grip every bit of your body and shake, now, you may have a new outlook on life because of that experience. Moreover, you may have a new outlook on death, too.

The way that you see death is likely very different know than it was when you were busy living life and raising your child. You can perceive death in several unique ways, though. For each person it is different and your perception may change from time to time. Let's examine the differences.

I Wish I Could Just Die To Stop the Pain

This is a very real feeling and one that can completely cause you pain, anguish and longing for many months or longer. As part of the grief process, there are various times when you may feel that life is simply not worth living. As we said, you should never put too much pain and suffering on your plate that it is so full that you cannot see tomorrow. Seek out help to work through thoughts of suicide, if that is where it comes from.

For others, though, the crying from the depth of your soul to make it just stop hurting is very real and very raw. It is part of the process of accepting death to feel that pain and in time, it will lessen, especially if you allow it to. For some, death looks like a better option than living through a life like this.

Death Isn't So Bad

Another way that people see death is in a lighter fashion. If they die, they die. There is someone in Heaven they want to see anyway. Death may not seem like something that is so morbid to them anymore. Instead, they may feel that it is something that is just going to happen, out of their hands and therefore not something to worry about or to be afraid of.

Not everyone will feel this way. Some may find that death is even more worrisome now. After all, can you accomplish all that you want to do in life before you die?

In either situation, the key is that death has changed and now, death may not seem so bleak as it once did.

Death Means Reunion

Even another way of looking at death is through rose-colored glasses. When you die, you will be able to reunite with your child. For those that believe in this type of after life, death does not seem like just a bad place at all. In fact, it may be a place to strive to reach simply so that they can get to see their child again.

Religion will play a role in the overall experience that you have in facing death. If you do not believe in an afterlife, you may not experience this level of understanding and acceptance of death.

Other Children Now

One of the key ways that life changes after the death of a child is the way that you interact with your other children. Your children are all important to you but your relationship with others may change drastically as you work through the loss of your child.

For example, for some people, other children become much more precious. They become a gift to be treasured and it may help you to find ways to make those baseball games and ways to get along with them if you did not do this before.

Other parents can take this to the extreme of feeling the need to protect their children. Some men will insist on protecting the remaining children seeing them at just as much of a risk as their other, lost child.

Many men find that the death of their child can be a way to reconnect to a child that they may not have had a good connection with prior. Through the grieving process, both can work to improve the relationship by being more open about feelings and about life expectations. At some point, it may be less important to get all A's on a report card and instead to spend some time watching a great movie or playing a board game. After all, time is limited.

Still other men may face guilt that is insurmountable and may position this guilt on other children. They may pull away feeling as if they hurt the other child too much or failed them by not protecting them. Men may also allow rage and pain that they feel to be relinquished on the remaining children. Why did they survive if the other did not? Most of this rage comes from the sense of failing to keep the child safe and failing, then, to be a good father. Of course, the children are not likely to see it this way and it is not true in the least.

When dealing with children after the death of one child, realize that they too are facing one of the most difficult times in their life and they often need support. While your pain may be too raw to offer them the support they need, you may be able to find ways to connect with them on a lower level so that they know you are there and that you too are hurting.

Your life will change when your child dies, but your life does not have to end or be less worthwhile. In fact, it may be an opportunity for you to be more than you ever thought you could.

Ways to Cope

When you lose a child, your body immediately goes into survival mode. Most of us are really never prepared to lose a child. Those of us who has a child that was terminally ill may have had taken the time to research how to cope when their child dies. For those of us who had a child taken suddenly, there is no time to prepare. So, we find ourselves grasping for straws and trying to learn how to cope with this loss.

This part of the book will identify different avenues of support and ways to cope. They are common knowledge to those of us who are several years into our grief. This information can be found online as well. However, trying to make heads and tails of this information after experiencing the loss of a child is much more challenging than it sounds. It is helpful if you have a friend or family member that can help you identify and research the different options. In my case, I was pretty much on my own. This kind of information would have been helpful for me, and I hope it serves as a beneficial source for you as well.

- Allow yourself to grieve. If there is any advice you
  men take from this book, let it be this. You have to
  grieve. I don't care how you do it, but you have to.
  Allow yourself to go through the different stages of
  grief. Cry if you feel like crying. Scream if you feel
  like screaming. You know the drill by now: Your
  game – your rules. The sooner you start to grieve,
  the sooner the healing process can begin.

- Talk. Find someone you can talk to. This can be a
  family member, a close friend, colleague, priest,
  deacon, etc. The important thing is to talk about what
  you are going through. Find someone who is a good
  listener. I am not much of a talker. Like most men, I
  tend to keep my feelings harbored up inside. However, I had a friend/colleague that I spoke to on a
  regular basis. It was good to just get things off my
  chest.

- Express yourself. As men, we are "expression –
  challenged." Expression will help in the healing
  process though. I took the creative approach. I express
  myself through writing. The five poems I wrote to
  Maci seemed very therapeutic. I also developed a
  website for one of the local Compassionate Friends
  chapters. All of these expressions contributed to my
  healing. Some people journal every day. Now that I
  am writing this book, I wish I had kept a journal. The
  key thing is to find that special something and start
  expressing yourself through it.

- Activity. If you are active, continue it. If you are not
  active, find something you enjoy doing. Exercise is a
  great stress reliever. Before I developed chronic knee

pain, I used to run all the time. Sometimes I go to the driving range and hit golf balls. I used to go to batting cages and "swing for the fence." It is important to take care of yourself physically. You are not going to want to do anything in the beginning, but you need to force yourself to do it. I promise it will make a difference.

- Work on being happy again. Oh yeah, this is a tough one. You probably feel like you will never be happy again. You will – in time. However, as soon as you are up to it, start trying to do some thing you enjoyed prior to the loss of your child. The first few times I played golf, I could not finish 18 holes. It took some time for me to not feel guilty about enjoying myself. Go out on dates or hang out with some friends. Whatever it was you enjoyed doing, start doing it again.

- Let yourself forgive yourself. When we lose a child, we immediately start blaming ourselves for things we did or we could have done. Being in the military, I was gone all the time. I wish I would have taken more time when I was at home to be with my kids. I often think if I would have called the kids and kept them on the phone for a few extra minutes, they would not have been involved in the accident. You have to let those feelings go. They are in the past. All we can do is focus on the future and how to be a better person. Losing a child often makes us better people.

- Do not let others blame you for the loss of your child. The problem is that we all feel like we need to blame someone. I blamed God and it took me several years to get through the blaming game. I have been blamed by others as well. I was 900 miles away, but yet I was the blunt of the blame. However, I forgive that person who blamed me for my daughter's death. This person said some horrible and hurtful things to me. I remained silent and took the verbal beating. It took me some time, but I now understand where those feelings and emotions were coming from. I can only hope that those words helped in his healing process.

- Support Groups. I am aware of a few support groups for bereaved parents, but I am biased towards The Compassionate Friends. It took me three months to find them, but they are the ones who saved my life. Whatever support group you decide, give it at least three visits before making a choice. This will be the one place where you go and everyone understands what you are going through. You can speak freely without being judged. I have found that the majority of the attendees are women. Once again we men have to set aside our egos and recognize it is ok to attend a support group. Some men have come to the meetings and said it is not for them. It is my belief that they are just trying to mask their emotions and being at the group makes it difficult to do that. They cannot "be strong" at the meeting. Guess what. It is not expected. All I can say is that it worked for me and it continues to work for me. Whatever works, right?

- Professional Grief Therapy. This is a tough one. I think every person that loses a child probably feels like they need professional therapy. I tried a grief counselor for a while and one visit to a psychiatrist. The problem I had was that they expected me to do most of the talking, and I was just not ready to talk about it. Sound familiar? However, some people have found emotional and psychological relief through professional therapy. Just because it does not work for one does not mean it will not work for the other.

I am sure you can do some research and find other ways to cope that I have not mentioned. As I prefaced in the book, I am not a medical professional. I am a father who has lost a child and just trying to share some pointers that worked for me. The key is to do something…anything.

Chapter 17

Support and Your Social Environment

The words, "support group" are likely to cause you some anguish. Who wants to sit in a room filled with other people and listen to them complain about the way that they feel about the death of their child?

Who wants to hear another person say, "I know how you feel" or "I am so sorry for your loss?" In most situations, these words do not even come close to being enough, but there are benefits to taking advantage of the support that is surrounding you.

For men, reaching out for support is one of the most challenging things they have to do. Asking for help is like admitting defeat. No one wants to admit they need help, but everyone that goes through the loss of their child will need help on both a professional and a personal level.

Ask yourself, who is your support system?

- Your spouse, children
- Your parents
- Your friends
- Others in your life that you are close to

These people will need your support as much as you need theirs. What is important to note here is that by giving support to your spouse or helping your other children to accept the death of their sibling, you are also working through your own grief.

Your support group will be specific to your situation. Therefore take a few minutes now to consider those around you and how they can and likely want to help you through this outrageous time in your life.

Support Groups

Support groups are another area that you need to take into consideration, even if you really do not want to. This is because even those that are okay in their stage of grief can use the help and support of someone that has been in their place already.

Support groups are unique and, unlike professional therapists, they have been there and done that, so to speak. The people within the group are people that have gone through and felt the exact same things you are feeling.

This really is a powerful tool because for many people, the words, "I know what you are going through" cannot mean anything unless they truly have been in the position that you have been in. Today, the death of a child is something as tragic as ever, but there may be people in your local area that have experienced it. This allows a unique opportunity for you. You can now take advantage of the experience of others as well as help others with your own grief.

As I have mentioned throughout this book, I am a true believer in a specific support group, one that can be found throughout the country and world. The Compassionate Friends or TCF, as it is often called, is one of the best choices available to you. Perhaps the most important part of using this or another similar group is the solace in knowing that there is someone out there that understands. You are not alone in your battle.

Support groups allow you to find a small bit of peace from the fact that someone knows what you are going through. You are not isolated from the world any longer. Because this is a self-help group, it feels more comfortable and easier to swallow than other professional services. Not only do you have the ability to sit and just listen, speak only when you want to and take all of the resources it offers, but it also provides an ear 24 hours a day, all year round.

I highly encourage you to get in touch with this group and allow it to become your source for healing, or at least understanding.

You can find a local chapter of the Compassionate Friends by visiting their website at: www.TheCompassionateFriends.com.

There are likely other groups in your area that offer help as well. You can find out more by visiting your local City Hall, Chamber of Commerce or by talking to your local counselors.

Professional Help

As I mentioned earlier in this book, I did seek out the help of a professional, who provided me with medication to get through the depression that I was in. Although I did not find my peace in this particular way, many have. You should consider talking to a professional especially if you are not able to use a support structure from your daily life or do not want to pursue a public group like support groups.

If you feel unable to cope with the intensity of your feelings, or you are unable to make your other relationships work, use these professional services. Therapists, social workers, psychologists and psychiatrists all offer opportunities for healing.

If you do use these services, I would highly recommend that you use a professional service that specializes in grief counseling. You need someone that you can feel comfortable with and that you feel has the experience to help you. The good news is there are many qualified individuals in most areas that can provide this for you. Do seek out a professional that can relate to your situation.

One of the benefits of seeking a professional is the privacy of this. If you do not want to tell your spouse you are seeking help, or do not want to let anyone know for that matter, you can do so. These professionals cannot talk about your case nor can they intervene in your private life. They are an outsider who you can spill your feelings to that will not have any impact on your life. In other words, crying in front of a professional may be easier than breaking down with your wife, especially if you are the type of person never to show emotion (Though you can do so!)

Although counselors can help, many are unable to help you to deal with the level of trauma of many parents who have lost children. As you can imagine, it is very difficult to relate to unless you have been there. For this reason, if you can, seek out the help of a support group where you are better able to have been say, "I know what you are feeling because I went through that, too."

Dealing with Social Situations

As you enter back into your life, you are going to meet people that you will see for the first time since your child's death. Many will avoid you. Others will say something that sounds so insincere such as, "I'm so sorry for your loss." In nearly all these situations, the problem is not that the individual does not want to help you, but rather they do not know what to say or how to say it. How could they? They have not been there!

These situations can be difficult to get through, nearly as difficult as having to tell someone you just met that you have three children but one passed away. These situations have to be dealt with on your own level, in your own way. You will need to consider the overall ability of the person to connect with you. Realize that they likely mean well but will unlikely know how to react.

Getting back into a social circle is important. It will allow you to get into the acceptance stage. The fact is, when you cannot hide behind closed doors any more, it is more likely than ever that you will push through the pain and find something else to think about. In most scenarios, social situations will be difficult at first, but will slowly improve over time. Give yourself time.

A Letter to My Daddy

Daddy,

It seems just like yesterday
When I was just learning to walk.
"Da-Da" was the first words I spoke
When I was learning to talk.

I still remember the times
When you would rock me to sleep.
You wiped away my tears
Every time I would weep.

You took care of my every need
But daddy, now it's my turn.
It's something new for both of us
Something we'll both just have to learn.

I know you thought I left this world
Before you could ever say goodbye.
But I was there in the hospital room
I held your hand as you cried.

I still have that tear
That rolled down your face.
It dropped onto my cheek
And in my heart it found its place.

You always called me "your little angel"
And it's true now more than ever.
I will be an angel watching over you
Until the last day of forever.

I know you don't understand
Why my life on earth had to end.
But God had a special reason
Another angel needed a friend.

Now I am up here with Papa
So please don't be sad.
He's so proud to have you as a grandson
I am so proud to have you as a dad.

So no matter how many years it will be
Until you are taken from this world.
Remember this for the rest of your life
I will always be "Daddy's Little Girl."

Your Little Angel,
Maci
"Kisses and Hugs"
Daddy
December 23, 2001

Chapter 18

Dealing with the Holidays

I touched on holidays in a previous chapter, but I think it has enough bearing to have a chapter of its own. Even as time goes by and the years pass us and the backpack of grief becomes lighter and lighter, the holidays will always be challenging.

The holidays are surrounded by people of cheer (most of the time). Although many people have experienced losses in their lives, very few have experienced the tragic loss of a child. It is impossible for those people to understand the deep void in our hearts.

As men, we go through the motions because that is what is expected of us. We put up the trees and hang the stockings. Putting up the Christmas lights is sometimes a blessing in disguise. It is our opportunity to be alone. There are times when we may even be able to shed a tear when sitting on the roof. You wives might find that there are more lights than usual on the house the first few Christmas'. Just smile and tell us they look beautiful.

Around Christmas (usually in November), you can rest assured that the topic of discussion at the monthly Compassionate Friends meeting will revolve around holidays. The newly bereaved parents are searching for the answers to getting them through the holiday season. The veterans in their grief are trying to give them answers.

Here lies the problem. What works for me will not necessarily work for you. What the veteran sitting next to me does to celebrate their holiday season is more than likely different than what I will be doing. As much as we would like to help, it truly is a trial by error, crapshoot, shot in the dark and any other cliché you can think of.

It seems like every year at the "holiday" Compassionate Friends meeting, I have been given a list and some brochures that provide ideas on how to cope with the holidays. I am not sure where the list originated from, so I cannot properly give credit to the source.

But if I had to guess, there were probably a group of bereaved parents who got together and shared their ideas over the years, and someone finally decided to capture them and put them on paper. To that person, I thank you. But just to be safe, I will source The Compassionate Friends since it came from the meetings I attended.

Listed below is a list of helpful suggestions that will hopefully help you get through the holiday season, and many of these ideas will work for other special occasions as well. Maybe there is one or two or a handful that jump out at you.

The nice thing is that there are no rules. You do what you can to get through this time of the year. For those of you who have attended one of the "holiday" Compassionate Friends meetings, this may seem redundant. For those who are reading this book and have never had the opportunity to attend a meeting, I hope it helps. If it helps at least one person, then it was worth the time it took for me to type it. Without further delay, here is the list:

1. Come up with a plan. The military side of me is always in the planning mode. I never thought I would use my military training during the holidays; at least not as a civilian. Sit down with your family and decide what you want to do for the holiday season and what each family member can handle comfortably. This is not as easy as it sounds. Remember, we all grieve differently and some will not be able to cope with what others think they are ready to cope with. As men, we will go with the flow. It's what we do. Just remember to take time to grieve in your own way on that day.

2. Remember I said there are no rules? I was not joking. There is no right way or wrong way to handle the day. Just handle it in your own way.

3. Some wish to stay with celebrating the holidays in their traditional way. The child would not want them to change anything. Others choose to change the way they celebrate. After all, it will never be the same. If the shoe fits, then by all means wear it. Once again, for us men, we will make the "shoe fit" regardless of the size.

4. Going over friends or family's house after the loss of a child is difficult. I am not even going to try to sugarcoat it. As much as we would like to talk about our child, you can believe that the subject of your child will rarely get brought up. People just do not

know what to say to us, especially during the holiday seasons. So, be prepared. If you want to talk about your child, then bring it up. Who cares what everyone else thinks. If you do not want your child brought up for whatever reason, just make sure your family and friends are aware of that prior to the visit.

5. Don't do too much. You simply will not have the energy. Take some time to reflect on past holidays when your child was with you. There were times in Christmas day when everyone was downstairs waiting on me to open presents. I would pull myself out of bed, cry for about 45 seconds, wash my face, and mosey downstairs. That was my time of reflection.

6. For some, you do not want to do too much. For others, you want to do everything. You just want to keep yourself so busy every minute of the day so that the day will just past and you can mark it up as a milestone.

7. Do something service related. Visit a homeless shelter and volunteer your services in the food line. Ask someone over to your house that would normally spend the holiday alone. Visit a nursing home and spend some time with the elderly.

8. If you feel like crying...CRY! You do not have to breakdown in front of everyone if that makes you uncomfortable. Excuse yourself for as long as you need. Those around you will understand. For us men, I think this is one of those very few occasions when we can cry and not be looked at as weak or a pillar of strength for our family. On the contrary, you will be

the hero, the sensitive husband who is there for his wife. What most will not realize is that you need this as much as your wife. It's your free pass – take advantage of it. The passes are few and far between especially as more time passes.

9. Do what is important to you and gets you through this day. More than likely, no one else is experiencing this grief. Make no mistake about it – you are in survival mode.

10. Try to get some rest leading up to the day. It is emotionally and physically draining. I say this with "tongue in cheek." Rest was the furthest thing from my mind. I could not sleep over the anxiety of the day. I just accepted the fact that it was going to be a tougher day than usual. Time to put on the mask and be the strong one.

11. Donate a gift or money to someone in need in memory of your child. The first year, I bought gifts and stocking stuffers for Maci. However, that just created another problem. At the end of the day, what would I do with those gifts? So, the following year, I bought a gift for a less fortunate seven year old girl and have been doing it ever since. In Maci's stocking, I place a pink rose because pink was her favorite color. It gets me though the season and I feel good that I can help another child. I know Maci would want it that way too.

12. For those who rely on their faith, attend a Christmas church service. Let God carry some of that burden.

13. Sending cards will be accompanied with another difficult decision. Do you add the child's name in the signature? If you feel like it, then do it. If you are undecided, then just sign the card with your last name (Merry Christmas from The Miller's). Remember, this is your game and your rules.

These are just a few ideas that will hopefully get you through the day. What works or doesn't work this year may have the opposite effect next year. Don't be shy about changing it up. Always remember that the anticipation of the day is normally much worse than the actually day. You make the rules – you can break the rules. Whatever helps you cope during this time depends on you and you only.

Chapter 19

Be Prepared for the Questions

Allow me to paint you a picture. You are very new in your grief or many years have passed since the loss of your child. You meet a stranger that wants to make small talk. One of the first questions they ask you is, "Do you have any children?" Then you can almost bet your paycheck that the next question out of their mouth will be, "How many do you have?"

If you have never thought about how you will answer this question, I can tell you how you might feel because it happened to me. You feel like you are going to go into cardiac arrest the first time you hear it. Your heart starts pounding. Your skin gets clammy. Your palms get wet. Your forehead breaks out in a sweat.

You normally do one and/or two things. You just look at the person as if they just asked you to provide them the answer to world peace. The second option is that you open your mouth to speak and realize you are stuttering. Neither one is worse than the other. Combining the two together makes you want to drop everything and run away.

So, how does one answer the question? I bet you know my answer by now. However you feel like answering. It's your rules. For me, it really depends on the person and the situation. You are going to have days when you want to tell the world about your child. Then you will have days when you prefer to keep their memory to yourself. Let your feelings guide your answers. The next question they will probably ask is their ages. If you include your child who has passed in either of these answers, be prepared to talk.

These questions will not be on life's final exam. There is no right or wrong answer. You get to choose how you want to answer the questions. My only advice is to be prepared for these questions because you will get asked them the rest of your life. So, maybe they are on life's exam, but the good news is that you will never fail. Your life, your test, your grading scale, and your rules!

Chapter 20

How to Answer

I have painted you a picture of what is going to happen throughout your life when it comes to people asking questions. Asking questions and being interested in someone is part of our human nature. As I previously mentioned, we get to control how the conversation goes by our answers. We are in the driver's seat.

I prepared you for a few critical questions in the previously chapter. Now I have to prepare you for the answers. You are going to hear the dumbest, idiotic, and ill-manner statements than you ever might have imagined. Allow me to introduce you to a handful:

"Well, they are in a better place."

"You can always have more children."

"I know how you feel. I had to put my dog asleep last year."

"It's been a few months. You should be over it by now."

"You are so strong. I don't know what I would do."

If you are reading this book, you have probably already heard at least one of these statements. The first couple of hundred times I heard these statements, I wanted to knock them out of the chair or send them through a wall. Here is how I personally wanted to respond to some of those statements:

"So, they are in a better place huh? Well, why don't you go and take your child and put them in a 'better place'?"

"What if I can't have more children? Even if I did, I would want them to be just like my child that is 'in a better place', and that will never happen."

"Are you really going to sit there and compare your pet to my child? All this time I actually considered you one of the intelligent ones. My mistake idiot!"

"A few months? How long did it take you to get over losing your child? Oh yeah, that's right, you never lost a child. I'll tell you what you can do with your few months!"

"You don't know what you would do? Well, you have two choices – kill yourself or learn to live with it. I chose the latter."

You can probably tell in my words how bitter I remain when I am confronted by these ignorant responses. It still chaps my butt when I hear these kinds of statements. It took a while but then I realized it was really not their fault. They have no idea what to say to someone who has lost a child. It's just not a natural thing to see a child die or to outlive your adult child. So, they say the first thing that pops into their head no matter how dumb and idiotic it may sound. Most would rather say something stupid and not realize it than to not say anything at all and have you think they did not care or have compassion.

About a year after my daughter passed, I attended the funeral of one of my army friends. I ran into another army buddy who I had served many years with and had not heard from him at all. He apologized for not contacting after Maci died. His reason was he just did not know what to say to me.

If you are reading this book and have never lost a child, here is the advice I offer to you. Sometime saying nothing at all is the best avenue of approach. However, if you are confronted with someone who has lost a child and feel obligated to say something, remember these five words: "I'm sorry for your loss." In these cases, normally less is more.

For those of us who have lost a child, the best thing we can do when faced with these statements is to just let it go. Normally the person who makes those statements is internally beating the crap out of themselves. Just smile and remember these two words: "Thank you." Then do these two words: walk away. It's not worth the energy to discuss it. Believe me – I have been down that road. Learn from my mistakes, and let it go.

Chapter 21

Breaking the Silence

As we mentioned earlier, the death of your child does not have to be finality, but a start for you and the rest of your life. You can move past the pain you feel and even use that pain in a better way in many ways.

Empowerment is perhaps the greatest lesson that you will learn from the grief you feel. Through grief, you will be able to go up the mountain of death and over all of the treacherous cliffs. Then, you learn how to climb down the steep slopes until you finally reach the bottom, living with acceptance. As you make this powerful trip, you will face the most treacherous of pain. The loss of your child can in fact strengthen you by providing you with insight and experience.

You know that the world is not ending when the boss is unhappy. You know that not making 20 hours of overtime this week is not going to ruin your life. You also are stronger to face other stresses and frustrations as they come to you over the course of the next years. You have this strength because, unlike so many others, you have already made the journey on the most difficult path. In doing so, you have built your strength.

Now, it is time for you to use that in some way.

Bettering the World through Your Loss

At this point in your life, suffering through the deepest of grief, it may not seem possible that you could actually find yourself sharing your pain with anyone else. You may not see it possible that you would be giving yourself to help others. Yet, through time and healing, you will.

There are many ways that you can share your experience to benefit others. Here are some things that you can do. Realize that helping others is a good way to move through the pain, eventually.

- Attend and participate in support groups. Become a leader to help others that are newly going through the pain.

- Offer your story to help others avoid the same situation. Talk to other families that lost their child to drunken driving, drugs, suicide or other more preventable death situations.

- Give lectures at schools and organizations about your child's loss and how it could have been prevented.

- Lobby and fundraise to help raise awareness of the illness that took your child and to help find a cure for the disease.

- Work in your religious organization offering help to other families going through grief.

- Share your story in a book that will help others.

- Work to help break society's ideals on how men grieve and show emotion.

- Establish a scholarship or have a plaque laid in the name of your child.

There are ways you can help make the memory of your child mean something. While you cannot change their death, you can work to make it mean something, in your own way. Take time to find the right way to make a difference based on your talents.

Chapter 22

The Heart Can Speak
Louder Than Words

I would be a rich man if I had a dollar for every time someone said to me, "I am sorry for not contacting you after I heard the news. I just did not know what to say and did not want to say the wrong thing."

I cannot blame them. After all, I used to be that person. Until Maci passed, I never realized how far a simple statement like "I am sorry for your loss" could go. Until I lost Maci, I never realized how important a hug could be. Until I lost Maci, I never understood the importance of a shoulder to cry on.

As I was putting the final touches on this book, I experienced firsthand the importance of a hug and a shoulder upon which to cry. In order to appreciate the experience, I must provide some details.

Every year, the 8th grade class at St. Jerome's Catholic School in Glendale, AZ adopts a refugee family. The purpose is to provide a new beginning for a family who has experienced years of pain and suffering while living in a refugee camp and now have a new start in the United States.

Each year, the students prepare a Mexican Dinner in which the proceeds are used to provide for the refugee family. These families come to us through Catholic Social Services with nothing more than the clothes on their backs.

This particular year we were blessed with a family from Burma. After eight years in a refugee camp, they finally made passage to the United States to start their new life all over again. The Lin family was comprised of the parents and seven children.

The first couple of visits brought furniture, a television, a computer and printer, microwave oven, and basic household items to furnish their three-bedroom apartment. Every Friday, the students, teacher, and a handful or parents visit the family bringing groceries, household goods, and anything they may need.

The students wanted to do something very special for Christmas. So, a few of us brave parents hauled 30 students to Wal-Mart and $4,100 and 18 shopping carts later (plus 8 bicycles), we had a magical Christmas planned for the family. We invited the family to the school to open all their presents. Then we let them really experience a piece of America by taking them to Peter Piper Pizza. Although their existed a language barrier between our students and them, there was no mistake that the love and joy between these children outweighed all the conflict this cruel world can sometimes dish out.

As you can imagine, we all became very close to our refugee family. While we were providing them with the basic needs, they were opening up their hearts to us. It did not take us long to fall in love with the parents and children of the Lin family.

One particular child that stood out was Andrew. Andrew was a 13-year-old child with a heart of gold. While coming home from school one day Andrew was hit by a car and died in the hospital the following day.

When I heard the news, I had the same reaction as everyone else who had heard. I broke down and wept. Although Andrew was going to be sorely missed, I wept more for his parents, knowing firsthand what it felt like to lose a child. I could not believe the emotions that were resurfacing after so many years.

The same day we heard the news, we paid a visit to the Lin family even though it was not our regular scheduled Friday visit. We walked into the apartment with the sound of soft music and pictures of Andrew displayed on the coffee table. Dad Lin (how I will refer to him) walked around the room and gave us all a hug. The rest of the family followed suit, and to those who could speak some English, thanked us for being there. After giving the family a hug, I settled in a chair in the corner of the room. All I could think about was that there had to be something I could do or say.

About this time, I looked over at the couch and saw Dad Lin sitting there and looking at the pictures of Andrew. There was nothing I could say to him because he did not speak or understand English. Therefore, I did the only thing I could think of. I walked over to the couch, sat down beside him, and put my arm around him. He reciprocated by placing his arm around me as well. After a couple of moments, he took the picture of Andrew, raised it to his forehead, and then began to weep. I place Dad Lin's head onto my shoulder and we both wept together for several minutes. After about 15 minutes, Dad Lin rose to go outside.

By the time Dad Lin had returned, my wife had showed a picture of Maci to the oldest daughter (who understood some English), and explained that I had lost my daughter as well. We asked her to translate that to Dad Lin. When she did, his reply was that his heart was sad for me. I replied and said I understood how he felt and that my heart was sad for him as well. Against all odds, we made a connection.

When something terrible happens to a friend or loved one, it is very difficult to say something that will make them feel better. Because of that, many choose to do nothing at all. Even though there was a language barrier between Dad Lin and me, embracing him in this strange new world was enough. My lips could not speak his language, but our hearts were in harmonic communication. If you are ever in a situation and you are at a loss for words, simply say, "I'm sorry" or provide a shoulder to cry on. You might be surprised how loud the heart can speak.

Always in Our Heart

Andrew,

The very first time we saw you
We knew you were special in every way.
Your smile had a way of lighting up the room
Like a sunbeam on a summer day.

Most of your life was a constant struggle
One thing we came to recognize.
One would never know the hardships you endured
Just by looking in your eyes.

In the short time that we knew you
You taught us lessons that will never part.
As we were teaching you to speak our language
You taught us to speak from our hearts.

We will never forget your last Christmas
And we can say without a doubt.
Sharing that special day with you
Reminded us what Christmas is all about.

We love our Friday visits
But they will never be the same.
We lost a special friend
But we know one day we will see you again.

Even though you had to leave this world
A part of you still continues to give.
Your heart still beats in another child
And in them you still live.

We will never ever forget you
As time continues to pass.
You will always live in the hearts and minds
Of our 8th grade class.

Mike Miller
In Memory of Andrew

Chapter 23

The Answer

For those who are newly bereaved, we all search for answers to the same questions:

- How am I going to get through this?
- When will I ever smile again?
- Will I ever get my energy back?
- Will I ever lose the feeling of not caring if I ever see the next day?
- Can I ever feel happy without feeling guilt?
- Will I ever be able to enjoy the things I use to enjoy?
- Will I ever be able to stop blaming God for taking my child?

Although there are so many more questions, I have found these are the most common questions we all want answers to. You may get many different answers. For me, and I think for most men, the answer is time. It may be a couple of years, five years, or even more. But eventually, you will begin healing and be able to move on with your life after this terrible loss.

Will you ever forget? Absolutely not! But eventually you start to cope with everyday life. Even after six years, I still have my bad days. However, it is comforting to know that they are few and far between. These days when I think of Maci, I think of all the good times we shared in her short life. I truly believe she is still with me in spirit and that gets me through most days.

The good news is that time is your friend. Yes, with time, we will eventually begin to experience the same joys we did prior to losing our child. I remember the first time I went golfing for the first time after Maci passed. I was over-whelmed with guilt and could not even finish the first nine holes. But I kept forcing myself to go and eventually I finished all 18 holes. Now when I play golf and observe the beauty around me (Arizona has some of the most spectac-ular courses), I think of Maci and feel she is my "angel caddie."

The bad news is that time is also your enemy. When you are newly bereaved (especially the first 2-3 years), you just want time to fly so quickly. It is in this period that you feel time practically stands still. Just getting out of bed and putting your feet on the floor takes more energy and you ever expended in a full day. Going through the day and acting is you are doing fine is even more emotionally drain-ing.

You will find that after a very short period of time, people have accepted the fact that your child – not theirs – has passed and it is time to move on. So, as men, as dads, we fake a smile and continue the role as the pillar in our family. The key thing to remember is that you have to grieve. I remember I use to sob in the shower. On holidays and special occasions, I would crawl out of bed and cry for a few minutes. Then I would wipe my eyes and go on through the day. I found time to grieve. Although I did not realize it at the time, I was healing with every passing minute of the day.

Support groups, family members, friends and anything you can do to get you through the day all plays a part in the healing process. These are things you can control. You will feel like you are grasping for straws every day. In the beginning, it will feel as if nothing is helping. I have listened to many bereaved parents from The Compassionate Friends that are still struggling after years of losing their child.

Time is their friend, but yet it is their enemy as well. No one can put a limit on the time that has to pass for you to start enjoying life again. If someone tries to specify a time, then they are the fools. The time that needs to pass is different for each and every individual. The misconception is that us men experience and require a smaller time frame than women to start the healing. This is so far from the truth. The fact of the matter is that most men grieve silently and in private. It is my belief that most of us dads require more time just for the fact that we do not allow ourselves to properly grieve.

This is what I say to anyone who reads this book – man or woman. Give us men a break. Remember we are trying to be strong for you, the other children, and the rest of our family and friends. We will lose friendships because we will not understand how to talk about it to other men. We will lose relationships with her family because we will just not under-stand how they can move on so quickly and expect us to "let it go."

Our relationship with our spouse or significant will probably weaken because our wives, our best friend in the world, does not see us grieving like she does. Trust me when I say we are falling apart inside. The pieces of our heart are so discombobulated that it feels as if it will forever be broken.

Remember, we are the ones expected to be strong. We are expected to be the pillar you can lean on every day when you do not have the energy to face the world. Please cut us some slack and know we are there being strong because we love you. We cannot afford to suffer another loss.

I have found that many marriages get stronger and many end up in divorce. As I mentioned, I am not a doctor or a professional grief counselor. I am just a man who has gone through a loss of a child and understand the struggles. I feel the reason so many marriages fail after the loss of a child is because of a breakdown in communication and the difference in the grieving process.

If there is anything you take from this chapter, I hope it is that you recognize dads need time to heal as well. We may require more time or less time. Regardless, we just need the time.

More importantly, we need our family, friends, co-workers, church congregation, coaches, teachers, everyone to just understand. And if we ever do open up to talk, please be there to listen without passing judgment. There will be times when we can no longer be the pillar and must bear our own cross. Just as Jesus himself needed someone to help bear his cross, there will be times when we will need that help as well. We probably won't ask for the help, and will just hope you can discern we need the help. Time will tell.

Chapter 24

Why Me?

Why me, God? Why did this happen to me? What did I do so wrong in my life to be punished in such a terrible way? Why are you doing this to me, God? If you have not asked yourself one or more of these questions or questions similar to them, then check for a pulse and make sure you are still alive. We have all asked one or more of these questions on more than one occasion. Most of us still ask these questions regardless of how long we are in our grief.

So, you are probably thinking to yourself that since I am writing this book and brought up the questions, then I have the answers. Sorry, I do not have the answers. If anyone had the answers to these questions, they would be a very wealthy person because many of us would empty our life savings for the answer.

So, why does something like this happen to someone like us? Why can't this happen to those hardened criminals or someone who deserves it? Here is what I choose to believe. Nobody and I mean nobody deserves to have their child taken from them. For those of us who have lost a child, we do not wish it on our worse enemies.

I believe that everything happens for a reason. I also believe that God will not put on us more than we can bear. I have to follow up saying I did not always feel like this. It was four years into my grieving that I finally let God back into my life. At the end of this chapter is a poem I wrote called, "The Day God Cried." Later, some very dear friends of mine put music to the poem. It was during this timeframe that I realized I no longer blamed God for taking my child. Some will never reach this spiritual realm. For those of us who do, we do not pass judgment.

There are still days that I wonder how I can bear the loss of my child. That burden does not ever go away, at least it hasn't for me or anyone else I have met. However, I have to believe that God gets me through those days. I am reminded of the "Footprints" poem and realize that the one set of footprints in my worst days is when God is carrying me.

So, why did it happen? Several paragraphs later, I still do not have an answer. However, there are a few of things that I do know. I have spoke to many fathers over the phone that just needed someone they could talk to. I never met these men in person and I only spoke to many of them one time. I have to believe that maybe I saved their life.

I have become more of a service-oriented person because I do understand this unique loss and can have compassion. I have written articles and poems that have helped others cope with their loss. I am now writing a book that will helpfully hope at least one person as they journey through this grief process. Am I patting myself on the back? NO! It is my way of answering the question, "Why?"

I believe that God has His reasons for taking my child. Maybe it has absolutely nothing to do with me. Maybe He was saving her from something even more terrible down the road. However, it is my decision on how I decide to live the remainder of my life. I believe that we all have a purpose in life. I have met too many beautiful and good people to believe we are all being punished. Only God has the answers, but we have the choice.

So, now we must decide and choose whether we are going to let this loss destroy us or if we are going to do something good as a result. It will take some time to reach this point, but I think we will all agree that the latter is the best choice. As far as I am concerned, I believe that Maci would want me to do something good and try to help other people. That's what she did in her short life. Now it is my turn to carry the torch.

Over six years into the grieving process, I find myself asking less "Why me?" questions and more "What can I do?" questions. Does this make me a saint? Should I get a special award? Does this mean I am special? Absolutely not. It's just my way of getting though life without my daughter. Remember, there are no rules. This is what works for me. My game – my rules.

The Day God Cried

God woke up this morning
Before the day could even start
An aching pain within His soul
Burdened with a heavy heart

Today he'd bring home a child
Long before her time
While heaven would rejoice for their new angel
Her daddy's tears would stream from his eyes.

When the time had come to call her home
Her daddy fell upon his face.
He cried out with angry tears,
"Please God, let me take her place."

God knew the meaning of suffering
He knew the pain that would come.
He knew what it was like to be a father
He knew the heartache of losing a Son.

God took her home on the wings of love
He whispered to her daddy in the wind,
"I'll take good care of your little girl
Until you see her again."

I know what you're going through
My arms are open wide
He bowed his head and shed a tear.
This was the day God Cried.

I love you and miss you baby!
"Kisses and Hugs"
Daddy
March 25, 2004

In Conclusion

Today is a new day. Today the book of your life has a blank page in it, one that you can fill with anything that suits you. You could spend today in bed, hiding under the blankets, at work buried in your work, or spend it with your family, sitting at the dinner table talking about....anything.

Each day is a new day, a new beginning and a new opportunity. No matter what stage of grief you are in, there are and always will be another opportunity for you to do more with your own life. You cannot change what has happened in the past, nor can you overlook the changes it has made in your day-to-day life. You are forever altered; someone different and mangled from where you used to be. Yet you can find a tomorrow with a new page waiting to be written.

There are no experts that can tell you when the pain will stop. There is no answer to the question, "Why?" You may never come to a definite place of understanding, but you can get to a place in your life where you make a difference.

You have three options, as we mentioned before. You can simply die and give in to the pain and sorrow that took your child. You could allow it to consume every moment of your day until you somehow lose your mind. Alternatively, you can allow acceptance to enter your life slowly and live your life the best you can.

The choice is yours to make. What would your child want you to be doing if they were here? Would you be playing a game of football in the backyard, tackling a new game for the gaming system or perhaps playing dress up where you all too willingly allow your daughter to plaster make up over your face?

If they were here right now, what would they want you to do with the rest of your life?

Tomorrow starts anew, a new day and a new blank page. You can do anything with that day. How will you spend your day? In sorrow or in love with the plan God has in store for you. Will you spend your day with a bottle of liquor in hand, hoping to make the pain go away? Will you take the next step of forgiveness for yourself, your God, your family and even for your child? Will you allow acceptance to enter your life, finally?

In your book, there are chapters that define your love for your child. There are exquisite details of your love and life with him or her there. Those chapters should be cherished. However, your book does not stop there. Your book is full with blank pages for tomorrows. Fill those pages in the ways that will make your child proud of you.

I urge you to seek help through support groups and support from your family. Take the time to realize that tomorrow offers opportunities, not more pain. You can get past today by looking towards tomorrow. Cherish your child and their memory, knowing you will see them again.

Remember, God has not finished with you just yet. In addition, your child was already as perfect as could be. That is why you are still here, while they are happily standing in Heaven, watching down at your right now. God has work for you to do and lessons for you to learn.

Then, on that day when you do see him or her again, you can sit on the beautiful bench in Heaven together and read the book of your life together, reliving the memories you both had and you sharing the chapters of your life that your child will be proud that you completed after they were gone.

Epilogue

Angels and Heroes

The focus of this portion is the only part of the book not devoted just to fathers who have lost a child. Although each one of you will be able to relate in your own way, this chapter is to educate those people in our lives on how they help us – knowingly or not, and it often is understood. This is my way of thanking those people who came into my life for a very brief period to provide a shoulder to cry on, a hand to hold, or just someone to be with me.

Most of my life, I believed in the fact that there existed some supernatural "beings" that watched over every person on earth. Everywhere you go, you can see books, bumper stickers, and songs about angels. Just the other day, I saw a bumper sticker that read, "Do not drive faster than your angel can fly." During the Christmas holidays, I hear the song with the lyrics, "I believe there are angels among us…" Many of us have experienced something in our lifetime that is unexplainable. How many times have you knowingly escaped death? How many times have you avoided that unavoidable accident? Has anybody ever grabbed your arm as you were about to walk across a busy street and saved you from being hit by on-coming traffic? Have you ever been down to your last penny in your checking account and then right at the nick of time receive a check in the mail that gets you through? Have you ever been "down in the dumps" and then receive a phone call from someone who managed to brighten your day? I could go on and on, but I think you get the point.

Many people believe in God, but do not believe in angels (at least the angels who live and dwell among us every day.) I believe in God and believe He watches over each one of us. However, I also believe that He has angels that serve as protectors and messengers that He sends in our time of need.

The angels that I want to talk about in this book are not the "supernatural" entities that we cannot see. The angels are real people who were there for me in my time of need. Some of these people are still in my life. Some were people who I saw for just a few minutes and then never saw again. Most of these people I do not even remember their names. Regardless of how long I knew the individuals, they all had a significant impact on my life.

The sad part and the reality of it all is that I did not even realize how much they truly affected my life until I started writing this book. To all of you who are reading this book and have been there with me through this journey, this is my way of paying tribute. Sincerely, I thank you.

In this part I will also mention some people in my lives who I consider to be true heroes. They could also be classified as angels, but there is something that separates them from the rest – something spectacular that stands out. These are the people that I look up to and respect. I admire their courage and tenacity. When faced against all odds, they managed to pull through. These heroes do not necessarily possess an incredible amount of physical strength. They are not geniuses.

They are not supermodels or professional athletes. They have not won the Nobel Peace Prize. However, they have traits that are even more appreciated and often overlooked in the qualities of a hero. They are courageous, honest, brave, selfless, and giving. The heroes mentioned in this book have well earned this title. I admire them.

As you read this chapter, I hope you will not take it out of context and read too much into it. As I share with you the small stories that make these people angels and heroes, I hope it will inspire each of us to strive to be someone's angel or hero. It is the greatest honor in which one can be bestowed. For anyone who has lost a child, we need our angels and heroes.

Angels

The Minister and his Wife. As I walked into the hospital upon arriving from the airport, a couple approached me and embraced me. I just fell into their arms and wept. They introduced themselves as a minister and wife of a local church in Louisville. I had never met them before that night, and have not seen them or spoken to them since then. At the time, it did not even cross my mind to how they knew who I was. As I look back, I would assume there are not too many people who walk into the hospital that late at night with luggage, and swollen red eyes.

They embraced me for just a few brief moments, introduced me to the hospital chaplain, and then were gone before I even realized they had left. At the time, I did not realize how important a role they played in my life. Here were two complete strangers who were there to help and provide support for a dad who had received the worst phone call a dad could receive. To them, I thank them for their compassion and kindness.

Two Special Friends. Throughout my life, I have never really had a plethora of friends. I have had many acquaintances, but not many who really fit into the "friend" category. Friends are people who stick with you in the good times and the bad. They may not always approve of the decisions you make in life, and they never pass judgment for the poor decisions we make. In the past 10-15 years, I have met and embraced the friendship of two special people – Dave and Kevin. I do not have to mention their last names because I am certain they will read this book and will know whom they are.

I met Dave in Officer Candidate School (OCS) in 1994. Those three and a half months were the most grueling times of our life and we leaned upon each other to get through them. Upon graduation from OCS, we continued together to our Basic Officer Course for the following six months. In those ten months, I developed a friendship with Dave that has lasted over the years. He has been there for me when I truly needed a friend. In the lowest points of my life, he was there to help me and just be a friend.

Dave and his family were my only friends that could make it to Maci's funeral. To hear what he had to go through to make it from Pennsylvania to Kentucky, and then turn around and go right back home is truly amazing. The interesting thing is that I did not even get a chance to speak to Dave and his family. After the service, I went to him, hugged him, and thanked him for being there. He could not even talk through the tears. He did not need to though.

Having him there was the best thing he could have done for me. It meant the world to me. If you did not know it then, you know it now. Thanks Dave.

Kevin and I served in the same unit for a few years. When he first came to our company, he took over my Platoon, and I took him under my wing. Even though he was a West Point graduate and I was an OCS graduate (quite the rivalry), we hit it off immediately. Kevin was one of those people that everyone naturally liked. I was lucky to have him as a friend. Over the years that we served together, he and I went through some things and relied on each other's friendship to get through them. I feel like I relied on him more than he did me, but I hope I was there when he needed a friend.

On the morning that Maci passed, Kevin was the first person I called; it was one of the hardest calls I ever made. Having to experience the loss of a child is the most painful thing we could ever go through. Almost equally painful is having to verbalize that pain for the first time. I needed Kevin to let others know about this loss. I needed him to be my messenger. Upon my arrival back home for the hospital, my mailbox was full of cards from people all over the world (those who I had served with in the Army) expressing their sympathy for my loss.

Kevin is one of those people who helped me throughout my journey. When I hit the bottom, he was there as a friend never passing judgment. I lost contact with Kevin for a few years, but recently was able to find him again. I am blessed to have him as a friend. Kevin, you know what I mean when I say, "I will kiss the ring." Thanks for your friendship.

The Nurse. I have never been to medical school. I do not know what is taught during the educational process or the internship. However, I have watched enough television to get an idea. Based on the treatment and bedside manners that my children received, I would have to say the television shows are accurate. I would venture to say based on the way we were treated in the hospital that the staff has to detach themselves from their jobs. They cannot get emotionally involved.

From one standpoint, I can agree with that. I am sure it is extremely difficult to work in a hospital (especially a children's hospital) day in and day out. However, I also believe that you have to have some extraordinary level of compassion when dealing with the children and parents. This was not our experience, except for one particular nurse.

I do not recall what the nurse's name was or what she even looked like. I just recall her being one of the younger nurses that was taking care of my son. She was always so kind and gentle when dealing with my son. When other nurses would rush through and yank off the bandages, she would take her time and make sure he was ok as she removed his bandages and cleaned his wounds. She made a difference in my life and an impact on my son's life.

If you are a nurse reading this book, you can learn something from the compassion of our nurse. Detach yourself if you must, but never lose that desire to help those who are in need. Thank you, nurse for being so kind, gentle, and patient with my son.

Concrete Soul. By now, you have read the poem titled, "The Day God Cried." This poem is very special to me, as it displays the time in my grief in which I actually started forgiving God for taking my daughter. To my astonishment and surprise, my wife, Lisa coordinated the efforts to have this poem turned into music. Nick and Keslie (Concrete Soul) combined their efforts and provided a beautiful piece of music that was blessed by the hand of God. To all three, you are truly angels from God.

Coach. After a few days in the hospital, we had a visit form a very special person – a well known basketball coach. I will not mention his name, but anyone familiar with basketball knows this coach. He coached for several years at the college level in Kentucky, went to the professional level for a few years, and then back to the college level in Kentucky once again. His visit brought a smile to my son's face – a time when smiles were few and far behind. Not only that, my son became the most popular patient in the hospital. The night shift nurses were so disappointed that they did not get the chance to meet Coach in person. Thank you Coach. You are a legend on and off the court.

Heroes

As I previously mentioned, it was very difficult for me to discern between who should be given the title of angel or hero. However, with much thought, I narrowed down the list.

The Compassionate Friends (TCF). I realize this hero is not an individual, but a group of individuals. It took me three months to find this group. If you have lost a child and have not attended a Compassionate Friends meeting, you need to look them up and pay them a visit. These people were my saving grace. There were people who were newly bereaved parents like myself, and those that were years in their grief (I call them veterans).

Being around TCF was the only place I could really share my feelings. I did not have to feel ashamed for crying. I could be honest with my feelings and what I was going through because the people in TCF either were going through it as well, or had already journeyed down that road. The true heroes in TCF are the veterans who continue to show up for the monthly meetings, even though they really do not need to for themselves.

The veterans do it for the people who are new in their grief journey and need to know that there really is life after losing a child. We needed to look at these people and know that one day we would be able to laugh again when we talked about our child. We needed them to put their arms around us and tell us it was going to be ok, because they really knew it would be. We needed them to tell us they understood how we felt, because they really did. I needed to know that my feelings for not wanting to live were normal and that many others had experienced the same pain.

God brought me to TCF, and it is this family that got me through the years. Below is The Compassionate Friends Credo in which we live.

We need not walk alone. We are The Compassionate Friends.

We reach out to each other with love, with understanding, and with hope.

The children we mourn have died at all ages and from many different causes, but our love for them unites us. Your pain becomes my pain, just as your hope becomes my hope.

We come together from all walks of life, from many different circumstances.

We are a unique family because we represent many races, creeds, and relationships.

We are young, and we are old. Some of us are far along in our grief, but others still feel a grief so fresh and so intensely painful that they feel helpless and see no hope.

Some of us have found our faith to be a source of strength, while some of us are struggling to find answers. Some of us are angry, filled with guilt or in deep depression, while others radiate an inner peace. But whatever pain we bring to this gathering of The Compassionate Friends, it is pain we will share, just as we share with each other our love for the children who have died.

We are all seeking and struggling to build a future for ourselves, but we are committed to building a future together. We reach out to each other in love to share the pain as well as the joy, share the anger as well as the peace, share the faith as well as the doubts, and help each other to grieve as well as to grow.

We need not walk alone. We are The Compassionate Friends.

The Mother. Although the children's mother and I were no longer married at the time of the accident, I was truly inspired by Rhonda's strength. Not only did she have to deal with her own physical injuries (which were extremely profound), she carried the mental anguish of knowing her children were lying in a hospital bed down the street from her. She relied on family and friends to keep her updated. The absolute worst thing was that she could not be there when Maci took her last breath and went to heaven. With the severe injuries that she obtained, Rhonda still managed to make it to the wake and to the funeral services.

I cannot imagine the physical pain that Rhonda was enduring. I was told that she signed a consent form stating that if the doctors could not fix her leg in surgery, they had her permission to amputate as a last measure. By the hand of God, they were able to wire the bones of her leg back together. However, this is what I admire about her most. Not only did she fight to keep her leg, she carried the torch for the winter Olympics in 2002. Her entire town recognizes that she is a wonderful person and a top-notch mother. I could not agree more. I admire her for her inner and outer strengths. She is a hero in the eyes of many.

My Son. You can say that I saved the best for last. As young boys, most of us aspire to grow up and be like our dads. We think our dads are the best in everything and can beat up every other kid's dads. For that matter, we even brag about it. Some of us young boys have gotten into fights defending our dad's honor. As for me, I am one of those that looked up to my dad for so many reasons. However, my son is my biggest hero. He displayed so much courage during those critical hours after the accident. Here are just a couple of incidents.

Soon after the cars collided, the car my kids and their mother were riding in caught on fire. A woman asked Michael Jr. if they needed help, and he nodded yes. She opened his door, pulled him out, and began to carry him out of harm's way. This is when he said, "Please put me down and get my sister and mom first." When the woman told me this, her eyes welled up with tears, and she said, "I have never met such a courageous and brave young man. You should be very proud of him."

Michael Jr. spent 11 days in the hospital. He experienced both emotional and physical pain. He was such a trooper and to this day, I do not ever remember him crying from the physical injuries. He is truly a wonderful brother, friend, and son. I feel extremely blessed to be his dad, and will always look up to him. Michael, I could spend every minute of our lives telling you how much I love you and how proud I am of you. Even then, it would not be enough time in our lives to truly show my love for you. Son, you are my hero.

I am sure that I left out many people who have been instrumental in helping me through this loss. I am fortunate to have all of my family and friends, and church members who were there to provide support and pray for me. Thank you for your love and support.

CPSIA information can be obtained
at www.ICGtesting.com
Printed in the USA
LVHW080117020620
657182LV00012B/438